THE FRAGRANCE OF EMPTINESS

The Fragrance of Emptiness

A Commentary on the Heart Sutra

Anam Thubten

Dharmata Press
Richmond, CA

The Fragrance of Emptiness

A Commentary on the Heart Sutra

© 2018 Dharmata Foundation, Richmond, California
Second Edition

All rights reserved. No part of this publication may be reproduced, stored in a retrieval system or transmitted in any form, or by any means (electronic, mechanical, photocopying, recording or otherwise) without the prior written permission of the author and the publisher.

www.dharmata.org

"From my heart, I rejoice that Anam Thubten Rinpoche has authored this fresh commentary, *The Fragrance of Emptiness*, in the English language on the profound sutras of the Great Mother Prajnaparamita, the Perfection of Transcendent Wisdom."

    Chakung Jigme Wangdrak Rinpoche, spiritual director of Abhaya Fellowship

"Anam Thubten reminds us with eloquence and heart that in emptiness there is an intrinsic compassion that wants the world to be okay, for self and for all beings, and this compassion is inseparable form and emptiness."

    Trudy Goodman, founder and guiding teacher of InsightLA

Contents

	Editor's Note	ix
	Author's Preface	xiii
	Heart Sutra Text	xv
1.	Introduction	1
2.	Thus have I heard...	17
3.	At the same time...	25
4.	The Path of the Bodhisattvas	33
5.	Then, through the inspiration...	45
6.	Madhyamaka Inquiry	69
7.	Then noble Avalokiteshvara...	79
8.	Form is emptiness...	97
9.	In the same way...	105

	Beyond Mind	115
10.	Negation, A Stage on the Path	117
11.	Negating Through Metaphors and Reasoning	133
12.	Thus, Shariputra, all phenomena…	155
13.	Therefore, Shariputra, in emptiness…	165
14.	No ignorance, no end of ignorance…	171
15.	No suffering, no cause of suffering…	185
16.	Therefore, Shariputra, since the bodhisattvas…	201
17.	Therefore, the great mantra…	207
18.	Then the Blessed One arose…	213
19.	Emptiness with Compassion-Essence	219
20.	A Daily Practice	229
	About the Author	237

Editor's Note

What you have in your hands is a compilation of extemporaneous oral teachings given by Anam Thubten over a period of several months in various settings. The original talks have been reorganized in some places to keep similar subjects together, and new content was added as Anam Thubten worked on this commentary. Since the topics were offered over a period of time, there is, of necessity, some duplication. This has been retained, along with Anam Thubten's unique and idiosyncratic use of the English language, in order to better offer an experience comparable to listening to the teachings in person. In some passages, you may also hear his humor and laughter about what might otherwise be a dense subject. While it is hard to capture the power of transmission that comes through oral teachings, if you can imagine Anam Thubten's voice speaking these words as you read them, you may get a hint of the experience that lies beneath the words.

During the rewriting and editing process with Anam Thubten, I observed first-hand his immense scholarship and love for the teachings. Often, he would quote spontaneously and precisely from a text that was written centuries ago. As he referred to ancient scholars and masters, I had the experience he knew them personally, despite the impossibility of that. And yet, on some level, he does know each of the ancients personally, as their teachings are so alive in his consciousness and heart.

In addition to his scholarship, Anam Thubten also displayed a meticulous attention to accuracy as he reviewed the text. Whether through researching the exact words of a quote, or removing a word that might misrepresent the truth, he consistently showed a high regard for using the correct language to convey somewhat difficult concepts. Any errors that may appear in this text, therefore, are solely due to the editor's transcription errors or editing mistakes.

Finally, it feels important to note that the level of wisdom and scholarship that Anam Thubten offers through this compilation may indeed become rarer and rarer in today's world. He offers not just an intellectual understanding of these teachings, but a fully lived and deeply felt expression of the experience they point to, creating a gift to all who come across this book.

The Indian texts often refer to commentaries as adding fragrance to gold. The scriptures are the gold, the words of the teacher add the fragrance that both intoxicates us

Editor's Note

and transforms our consciousness. May all who read this compilation be blessed by the *fragrance of emptiness.*

Note on Foreign Languages

Throughout his teaching, Anam Thubten often uses Tibetan words or phrases, which he then translates into English. In many cases, we have kept the Tibetan. The style we use is *Phonetic Pronunciation (Wylie Transliteration).* While Anam Thubten's pronunciation is a dialect of Tibetan from Golok, in this text we are using phonetics for Lhasa pronunciation.

There are also many references to Sanskrit terms and especially Sanskrit texts. For simplicity, we have omitted diacriticals from the Sanskrit, and used commonly accepted pronunciation; for example, *ś* is represented as *sh* (*śūnyata* becomes *shunyata*), and the Sanskrit *c* is represented as *ch* (*bodhicitta* becomes *bodhichitta*). In a few instances, a Pali term is used, and the language is indicated. Only the first occurrence of any Tibetan, Sanskrit, or Pali word is italicized. Following an accepted convention, *Madhyamaka* refers to a philosophical school while *Madhyamika* refers to people who practice it.

Laura Duggan

Author's Preface

The *Heart Sutra* is the essential synthesis of all the *Prajnaparamita Sutras,* and has been a catalyst for the awakening of many people in the past. *Prajnaparamita* means the transcendent wisdom, or the perfect wisdom, or the highest wisdom, which is the realization of the great emptiness.

The Dharmata community has a leadership program that lasts for two years. During the course, we choose some Buddhist classical texts as part of the curriculum and we study them thoroughly. One of them is the *Heart Sutra*. I gave quite an extensive commentary on it in 2016 and felt so fortunate to have an opportunity to share my knowledge about it with my friends. This sutra has a special place in my heart and has been the best companion many times in my life. This book is based on my oral commentary on the sutra during the classes.

My wish is that this book will help others to love and understand this extraordinary sutra, which has been the source of light to many. My intention behind publishing this book is to help people understand the profound wisdom of the *Heart Sutra*, wisdom that does not reject the existence of the world and the karmic law of cause and effect, past, future, nirvana, samsara. It only negates the *svabhava*, or intrinsic nature, in all things.

Anam Thubten

Heart Sutra Text

Thus have I heard: Once the Blessed One was dwelling in Rajagriha at Vulture Peak Mountain with a great gathering of monks, nuns, and bodhisattvas. At that time, the Blessed One entered the samadhi that expresses the Dharma called "Profound Illumination."

At the same time, noble Avalokiteshvara, the Bodhisattva Mahasattva, while engaging in the profound transcendent wisdom, clearly saw the five skandhas to be empty of nature.

Then, through the inspiration of the Buddha, venerable Shariputra said to noble Avalokiteshvara, the Bodhisattva Mahasattva, "How should a son or daughter of noble family train, who wishes to follow the profound path of transcendent wisdom?"

Then noble Avalokiteshvara, the Bodhisattva Mahasattva, said to venerable Shariputra: "O Shariputra, a son or daughter of noble family who wishes to follow the profound path of transcendent wisdom should see in this way: See the five skandhas to be empty of nature.

"Form is emptiness. Emptiness is form. Emptiness is no other than form; form is no other than emptiness. In the same way, feeling, perception, formation, and consciousness are emptiness.

"Thus, Shariputra, all phenomena are emptiness. They have no characteristics. There is no birth and no cessation. There is no impurity and no purity. There is no decrease and no increase.

"Therefore, Shariputra, in emptiness, there is no form, no feeling, no perception, no formation, no consciousness; no eye, no ear, no nose, no tongue, no body, no mind; no appearance, no sound, no smell, no taste, no touch, no phenomena; no quality of sight and so on, until no quality of thought and no quality of mind-consciousness; no ignorance, no end of ignorance up to no old age and death, no end of old age and death; no suffering, no cause of suffering, no cessation of suffering, and no path; no wisdom, no attainment, and no non-attainment.

"Therefore, Shariputra, since the bodhisattvas have no attainment, they abide by means of transcendent wisdom. Since there is no obscuration of mind, there is no fear. They transcend falsity and attain complete nirvana, passing beyond the bounds of sorrow.

Heart Sutra Text

"All the buddhas of the three times, by means of transcendent wisdom, fully and clearly awaken to unsurpassable, true, complete enlightenment.

"Therefore, the great mantra of transcendent wisdom, the mantra of great insight, the unsurpassed mantra, the mantra that equals the unequaled, the mantra that calms all suffering, should be known as truth, since there is no deception.

"The mantra of transcendent wisdom is said in this way:

> Gaté Gaté Paragaté Parasamgaté Bodhi Svaha

"Thus, Shariputra, the Bodhisattva Mahasattvas should train in the profound transcendent wisdom."

Then the Blessed One arose from that samadhi and praised noble Avalokiteshvara, the Bodhisattva Mahasattva, saying, "Good, good. Thus it is, O son of noble family, thus it is. One should practice the profound transcendent wisdom just as you have taught, and all the Tathagatas will rejoice."

When the Blessed One had said this, venerable Shariputra and noble Avalokiteshvara, the Bodhisattva Mahasattva, that whole assembly, and the world with its gods, humans, asuras, and gandharvas rejoiced and praised the words of the Blessed One.

I

Introduction

Everyone of us feels that there is a "me" as the main actor on the stage of life, and that the whole show lies on a solid ground. Then there is the world out there with its value system that we all follow in one way or another. We agree that the way we perceive things is true, and together we construct a consensus reality. This behavior is part and parcel of our world, and we cannot function as a species if we haven't developed it. This whole process is what Mahayana regards as the relative truth. Relative truth is not to be rejected. Yet if we only see the relative truth and believe that it is the whole picture of reality, it becomes like a big dream in which we continue to live, or a cosmic prison in which we're trapped without even knowing what is happening.

Life starts as a gift from the universe that comes with pain and difficulties. It doesn't spare anyone, no matter how lucky, including the rich and powerful ones. Our response to suffering is individual. Some learn lessons from it. Others wallow in it, perpetuating their addiction to misery. Our conceptual apparatus is always trying to figure out the primary factor for all our woes. It doesn't always perform good work in assessing the situation. It might see that uninvited mishaps and unfavorable circumstances are the factors that cause our unhappiness. With this notion, we're often trying to be in control of our own life and the greater world, which is an impossible task, and we suffer endlessly from hope and fear, until some big awakening strikes us from within.

Once we deeply inquire into the relative truth, it becomes more and more groundless and illusory. With such insight, we begin to realize that the main source of human woes is ignorance, or blind faith in the validity of the relative truth. Seeing the groundlessness of the relative truth is the ultimate truth. This should remind us that the ultimate truth is not some kind of eternity that lies separately above or a soul-like essence of all things. Such ideas are a form of eternalism. The Buddha's teachings transcend both eternalism as well as nihilism. Due to our tendency to fall into the trap of those two isms, many people don't understand—or they misunderstood—the

Introduction

Buddha's teaching. This is not just a problem among non-Buddhists but among Buddhists as well.

Awakening to the ultimate truth can lead us to profound happiness, which no amount of money can buy. This is not a false promise. Enlightened yogis demonstrated this in their lives. They remained happy amidst all kinds of situations. The mighty kings and emperors of the past couldn't acquire this state by being powerful and smart.

If this is so, why are more people not rushing toward such awakening? It might not be that easy for us to just let go of our attachment to relative truth overnight and become enlightened the next morning. In some sense, our human ego is terribly afraid of letting go of what is known and familiar to us, and becoming great inside. That would be like trying to leave one's planet, falling into an endless space where there is no sign of a possible place to land. So it feels safer to stay on the same planet even if that might not be very idyllic.

Buddha himself came up with a name for the ultimate truth: emptiness. Even such a word can give us chills, although the word means something utterly different than what one might assume. It takes a long time for a culture to understand the true meaning when such a word enters into its consciousness as a new concept. This happened almost every time the Mahayana tradition went into a new culture. Even ancient Buddhist followers misunderstood emptiness through the lens of their cultural background before they began to realize what they were dealing with. As almost an unconscious strategy, sometimes people turned emptiness into some external omnipresent thing that they could simply worship, while feeling that they didn't have to let go of anything, including all the illusions that they were attached to. This turned out to be a form of wishful thinking. Cheating on enlightenment never works—either we let go, or we forget the whole enlightenment thing.

When people started translating Eastern spiritual writings into English, some translated *shunyata* as *openness*. Such translation completely missed the point, even though it sounds very nice. It gives us the notion that we don't have to let go of anything and can still find inner liberation. Tibetans and Chinese faithfully translated the word *shunyata* as *thong nyi (stong nyid)* in Tibetan, and *kong* in Chinese. The etymology of both translations has the direct connotation of emptying or voiding rather than openness or something like "everything is hunky dory."

Some translators thought that the word *emptiness* implied nothingness, a blatant nihilism, and turned people away from these sacred teachings. The truth is that emptiness is far from being nihilistic. In the end, it doesn't reject anything; it simply helps us to lose our tendency to reify things or take things too personally.

The wisdom of emptiness is the foundation of the Mahayana traditions, such as Vajrayana and Zen. We cannot understand these traditions unless we have quite

Introduction

a clear comprehension of emptiness. Since Buddhism is a nondual tradition, the tantric deities in Vajrayana are not to be regarded as individual supernatural beings who reside outside ourselves, like God in the Abrahamic religions, but as allegories representing emptiness and the awakening to it. Regarding the deity as a separate and individual entity is considered wrong understanding according to Tantric Buddhism. This is why it is so important for people to know the true meaning of emptiness, especially for those who are practicing Vajrayana, as well as Zen.

Even though emptiness is mentioned in various sutras, it is emphatically taught in the *Prajnaparamita Sutras*, and masters such as Nagarjuna further explained it in the Madhyamaka *shastras*. The *Heart Sutra* is considered a sutra that captures the essential wisdom of all the *Prajnaparamita Sutras*. It has been translated in many languages. Chinese, Tibetan, Japanese, and Korean monasteries use the *Heart Sutra* as one of their main liturgies. There have been numerous commentaries on it from the point of view of general Mahayana as well as Vajrayana. Those who know its meaning find it most beautiful and profound, while others find that it is quite obscure with all its nonsense utterances.

Recitation and Reading

Before we start studying the *Heart Sutra*, we might like to chant it because as we chant, we develop an affinity and feeling toward this sutra that will help us understand its wisdom. Not only do people chant this sutra, they also write it down. Some Tibetans are excellent calligraphers, so they write the entire sutra in beautiful calligraphy as a way of getting to know its depth. There is also a long tradition of carving the sutra in stone. All these practices are a means of developing an affinity and devotion toward this sutra, which can help us understand it not just conceptually but experientially.

Recitation and reading of sutras have been a large part of spiritual practice in Buddhism. In the past, some individuals made a commitment to recite a sutra once a day; sometimes it was quite a long sutra. Growing up in Eastern Tibet, I knew one lama in my community who recited a very long liturgy known as the *Sutra of Great Liberation*. Every day, he found time here and there to recite the whole text, reading it at a very fast speed. Such practice has deep roots in certain Buddhist traditions that emphasize the ten Dharma activities, which include reciting sacred scriptures and writing them down.

In the Tibetan tradition, people used to go into solitary retreat and sometimes read the entire 100,000 verses of the *Prajnaparamita Sutra*. Machig Labdron, the twelfth-century

Introduction

female mahasiddha, was known for her love of the *Prajnaparamita Sutra*. She was said to be an unbelievably fast reader; not even the well-trained monks were able to keep up with her. Traditionally, monastics and others were often invited to recite longer or shorter versions of *Prajnaparamita Sutras* for various occasions, such as healing illness, as a ceremony for the dead, and other occasions. In the early days of Machig Labdron's life, she was invited by others to recite the entire 100,000 verses for their benefit. It is said that at one time, she recited the *Prajnaparamita Sutra* and had an awakening while she was reading the *Chapter of the Maras*.

We hear quite interesting and very wild stories about people who became awakened by reciting the sutras or sometimes just by overhearing a few lines from the sutras. The Zen master and sixth patriarch, Huineng, was delivering firewood and heard a monk reciting the lines from the *Vajracchedika*, the *Diamond Sutra*. The Zen master became enlightened, had an awakening, just because he heard the monk chanting a few lines from the *Diamond Sutra*.

As lay people in the world today, we might not have the time to recite a long liturgy. Nevertheless, having some prayers and chants will enrich our spiritual practice. The *Heart Sutra* is an amazing sutra to recite either in daily life or on special occasions, such as weddings, funerals, and celebrations. There are many people whose interior lives have been transformed through chanting this sutra.

In some ways, this is a very difficult sutra, one that can conjure up some intricate philosophical ideas. On the other hand, its main purpose is to wake us up from the world of illusion. So we can chant it as a nonconceptual prayer to let go of our cherished illusions, without worrying about the philosophical components.

Sutras as the Buddha's Words

Before we look at this sutra in detail, we might like to understand more about sutras in general and their relationship to the Buddha's teachings. In Buddhism, generally a sutra is considered a scripture attributed to the Buddha himself. Today, these sutras are found in Pali, Tibetan, and Chinese canons. The sutras are revered not only as the primary basis of Buddhist teachings, but also as sacred objects that represent the Dharma and true words of the Buddha. In the Tibetan culture, there is a belief that sutras are so sacred that one is not even allowed to put sacred statues on top of them.

People often chant the sutras as a means of karmic purification; as a way of accumulating *punya*, or merit; as well as on certain occasions for various purposes to fulfill the spiritual needs of society.

INTRODUCTION

People also quote lines and verses from sutras as the true words of the Buddha to make a point in their lectures and writing. Yet even though all sutras are sacred, we don't have to take every word literally. Some of the Buddha's teachings have a radically contrasting message from others. This is not because Buddha was saying contradictory things; rather, he gave teachings that resonated with an audience at a particular time and place.

Buddha was a master of *upaya*, skillful means. He knew how to communicate with others and often used his wisdom to say only what people could handle. He might have felt that others would run away if he spoke the truth in an uncompromising fashion. Yet there were also times when Buddha was fierce if he felt people needed to hear a truth that might be challenging or inconvenient for them. These skillful means that Buddha used remind us that we don't have to hold everything being said in the sutras as absolute truth.

Emptiness in the Sutras

There are different genres of sutras that share a common and special emphasis. The *Prajnaparamita Sutras* deal particularly with the topic known as *shunyata*, or emptiness. While the Mahayana idea of emptiness is thoroughly elucidated in the *Prajnaparamita Sutras*, emptiness is also taught in many other sutras, including the Pali sutras.

The tenets of various schools do not necessarily agree with each other about how to explain the subtle point of emptiness. This was originally the case in India, and then the Tibetans further developed different philosophical systems on this topic. Yet all the Mahayanists go back to the *Prajnaparamita Sutras* as the true source of the doctrine of emptiness.

Emptiness is also one of the most important concepts in Vajrayana. As a form, Vajrayana may look very different from the general Buddhist path, which is sometimes known as Sutrayana. Yet they are completely intertwined with each other. There is no Vajrayana without Sutrayana. The Sutrayana is like the root, and the Vajrayana is like the flower produced from it. Some people might hold the notion that Sutrayana and Vajrayana are totally unrelated paths, and that they could skip Sutrayana completely and practice Vajrayana. This can be quite dangerous and may lead one to miss the opportunity to study important philosophical systems, such as Madhyamaka, which hold such rich teachings on emptiness and many other important topics.

Versions of Prajnaparamita Sutras

In the Tibetan version of the Buddha's canon, there are many *Prajnaparamita Sutras*. Usually we say there are three versions of the *Prajnaparamita Sutras*: the extensive one, the medium one, and the short one. The extensive one is called *bum* (*'bum*) in Tibetan, which means 100,000, because it has 100,000 *shlokas*, or verses. The medium version is called *nyi tri wa* (*nyi khri pa*), the *Prajnaparamita Sutra* that has 20,000 verses. Then the short version of the *Prajnaparamita Sutra* is called *gyé tong wa* (*brgyad stong pa*), which means 8,000, because it has 8,000 *shlokas*. The *Heart Sutra* is shorter than any of these, and is considered the sutra that synthesizes these three versions of *Prajnaparamita Sutras*.

One can say the shortest *Prajnaparamita Sutra*—or maybe not even a sutra but the word—that can express the profundity of all these sutras is the letter or syllable *Ah* (ཨ). There is an explanation about *Ah* as the ultimate mantra that expresses the great emptiness. *Ah* is a very important syllable in the Tantric tradition; Tantric *sadhanas* use *Ah* as a mantra to chant, and also as an object of visualization. It expresses the great emptiness as well as the *unconditioned*, the truth that goes beyond all worldly limitations.

Today we find two main versions of the *Heart Sutra*: the Chinese version and the Tibetan version. They are quite similar to each other. The Chinese version has a short form and a long form, and the short form seems to be very popular.

The Tibetan version has an opening saga describing Buddha residing at Vulture Peak Mountain, and at the end, Buddha gives words of affirmation to the dialogue between Avalokiteshvara and Shariputra. In the short Chinese version, Buddha and the legend at the beginning are not included; the sutra contains only the dialogue between Avalokiteshvara and Shariputra.

Originally, the *Heart Sutra* was composed in Sanskrit. In general, the same sutra can have slightly different versions, depending on the translator and the period when the sutra was translated. You can see this especially in the Chinese versions of the *Heart Sutra*. Also, some translators were faithful to the original verses, while others were more concerned with the meaning rather than the literal words, and took the liberty to change the language to capture the meaning, rather than translate word by word. This kind of translation is called *don gyur* (*don bsgyur*) or *meaning translation*. The fourth-century Central Asian translator, Kumarajiva, for example, was concerned mainly with the meaning rather than the literal words in his translations.

Commentaries on the *Heart Sutra*

There are many commentaries on the *Heart Sutra*, written by both Indian panditas, such as Vimalamitra, as well as by Tibetan masters. It's quite interesting to find that Buddhist masters have written commentaries on the *Heart Sutra* from different points of view—Dzogchen and Vajrayana, as well as Sutrayana. For example, the early Indian Dzogchen master Shri Singha wrote a Tantric commentary on the *Heart Sutra*. The *Heart Sutra* is an amazing teaching that can

INTRODUCTION

be interpreted in many ways, depending on where you are on your path.

There are a few Tibetan commentaries on the *Heart Sutra*. One is by Taranatha, a great sixteenth-century Tibetan teacher and scholar. Another is by a Mongolian scholar, Alaksha Ngawang Tendar, who was educated at a Tibetan monastery. He lived a few centuries ago, and although he was a Mongolian, he became the most prominent scholar in Tibet during his lifetime. He wrote many commentaries on various teachings and root texts using the Tibetan language. This was considered unique because while many Mongolian monks came to Tibet to be educated in Tibetan monasteries, very few had the linguistic ability to write in the Tibetan language on a par with native Tibetan scholars. As twentieth-century scholar Gendun Chöpel once said, "Alaksha was the only Mongolian who could write in the Tibetan language like a Tibetan."

When you compare the *Heart Sutra* commentaries by Taranatha and Alaksha, they sound totally different, with somewhat contrasting views on emptiness. This is because Taranatha came from the Tibetan Madhyamaka school *zhen tong (gzhan stong)*, while Alaksha came from the school known as *rang tong (rang stong)*. These schools don't agree with each other philosophically.

In general, the Tibetan commentaries tend to be extremely academic and detailed. Sometimes it is very difficult to comprehend the Tibetan commentaries because you have to be familiar with so many Buddhist philosophical treatises, such as Madhyamaka, Abhidharma, Prajnaparamita shastras, and so forth. For example, the five *skandhas* mentioned in the *Heart Sutra* are extensively taught in the Abhidharma, and we would need to study the Abhidharma in order to have a full understanding of them. Since many of the Buddhist teachings are interconnected with each other in this way, the traditional Gelugpa monasteries study the five great treatises, such as logic (*pramana*), Prajnaparamita, Madhyamaka, Abhidharma, and Vinaya; and the Nyingma monasteries study the topics in the authoritative thirteen Indian treatises, known as the Great Thirteen Texts, *zhung chen chu sum* (*gzhung chen bcu gsum*).

In this commentary, we are trying to have a little bit of balance—not being too academic and conceptual, but at the same time, trying to understand this sutra from the point of view of the Tibetan panditas.

Three Wheels of Dharma

Let's talk a little bit about the time of the Buddha and what he taught. This will help us understand where the teachings of the *Prajnaparamita Sutras* fall in terms of Buddha's life and his teachings.

Introduction

Mahayana Buddhists hold the concept that Buddha gave countless sermons and sutras, which can be categorized into the three turnings of the wheel of Dharma. This concept is held only by Mahayana Buddhists. Non-Mahayana traditions believe there is a "turning of the wheel of the Dharma" but not three turnings.

The wheel, or *chakra*, which symbolizes the Buddha's teachings, is an important symbol in Indian spirituality. In the Indian context, the chakra is a miraculous weapon used by the Chakravartin, the universal queen or universal king. When she throws it, the wheel miraculously flies around and conquers all the other forces, bringing the whole world under her power. The Buddhists have an extensive explanation for why this allegory is a perfect symbol for the Buddha's teachings. They say when you practice the teachings of Buddha, the forces of Mara—the force of *kleshas*—are conquered, and you attain enlightenment, which is the ultimate triumph.

The first turning of the wheel of Dharma is the sermon on the Four Noble Truths. The second turning of the wheel contains the teachings on the great emptiness. The *Prajnaparamita Sutras* can be regarded as the sutras that belong to the second turning of the wheel of Dharma.

The third turning of the wheel, called the "teachings on the utter distinction," contains many other topics, such as *tathagatagarbha*, or buddha nature. In this third cycle, Buddha distinguished phenomena into three categories:

the imaginary, or mentally constructed (Sanskrit: *parikalpita*), the dependent, or relative (Sanskrit: *paratantra*); and the absolute, or ultimately existent (Sanskrit: *parinispanna*).

The three turnings of the wheel of Dharma can be further categorized into two categories: the interpreted, or indirect, or provisional teachings, *drang don (drang don)*, and the definitive or ultimate teachings, *ngé don (nges don)*. The provisional teachings are considered sutras that don't contain the ultimate truth or cannot always be taken literally. For example, in the provisional teachings, Buddha said there is a self. The definitive teachings reveal the ultimate truth, so they don't need any further interpretation and can be taken literally.

The Gelug tradition thinks that the first and third turnings of the wheel are provisional teachings and only the second wheel falls into the definitive teachings. Scholars in other Tibetan traditions, such as Nyingma and Jonang, hold a different opinion; they regard only the first turning of the wheel as provisional, and the second and third belong to the definitive teachings.

However, all the traditions agree that the *Heart Sutra* and Prajnaparamita belong to the ultimate or definitive teachings, so we can trust it word for word.

Now let's look at the text of the *Heart Sutra* itself.

2

Thus have I heard...

Thus have I heard: Once the Blessed One was dwelling in Rajagriha at Vulture Peak Mountain with a great gathering of monks, nuns, and bodhisattvas. At that time, the Blessed One entered the samadhi that expresses the Dharma called "Profound Illumination."

It seems that when Buddha taught, nobody actually wrote his teachings down. Instead, his students, especially Ananda, memorized many of the Buddha's teachings. Shortly after Buddha's passing away, Mahakashyapa decided to hold the first Buddhist council and summoned five hundred *arhats* to come together. One reason he did this was to preserve Buddha's teachings. It is said that another reason Mahakashyapa called the council was because at that time, monks and nuns only emphasized meditation; there was no interest in studying the teachings. This became problematic, and by creating the canon, they could now study the Buddha's teachings.

At the council, it is said that the whole assembly of monks came together to collect all of the sermons given by Buddha, which were then categorized into the three baskets, or *tripitaka* in Sanskrit: Vinaya, Sutra, and Abhidharma. At the meeting, Ananda recited Buddha's sutras from memory. Upali recited the Vinaya and then Mahakashyapa collected the Abhidharma.

Ananda was a very important individual for his role in preserving the Buddha's teachings. He spent many years being close to Buddha. Ananda was Buddha's relative as well as his attendant, and was responsible for inspiring Buddha to teach many of the sutras. He had an amazing mental power of recollection, and was able to remember almost everything that Buddha taught.

It is said that when Ananda stood in front all of the monastics and arhats at the first Buddhist council, he remembered the qualities of the Buddha, and his eyes flowed with tears; he joined his hands together and began reciting in a beautiful melody, "Thus have I heard..." In the *Heart Sutra*, "Thus have I heard..." refers to Ananda recalling the Buddha's words.

During his life, Buddha traveled to different regions in India, offering many sermons. At the time of the *Heart*

Thus have I heard...

Sutra, Buddha was residing at Vulture Peak Mountain in Rajagriha, a region in India. Some say this mountain is called Vulture Peak Mountain because the shape of the mountain resembles a vulture. Vulture Peak Mountain is considered a holy site for Buddhists because of the legend that Buddha taught all the *Prajnaparamita Sutras* there.

Right Recipients for Emptiness

This *Heart Sutra* verse says that Buddha was residing at Vulture Peak Mountain, presiding over a great gathering of monks, nuns, and bodhisattvas. The Tibetan commentaries say that the words "monks and nuns" don't refer to just any monks and nuns but to awakened monks and nuns, or arhats.

The idea is that emptiness, *mahashunyata*, is so profound it requires a special audience. For instance, some Buddhist texts say that the teaching on emptiness is not for everybody and requires a special mental capacity or readiness to hear it, contemplate it, and love it. These texts even lay out a list of signs to describe individuals who have the mental capacity to hear the truth of emptiness.

For example, in his text, *Madhyamakavatara*, Chandrakirti said,

> *Even while they are ordinary individuals,*
> *by hearing emptiness, bliss will rise inside them*
> *again and again.*
> *From such utter joy, their eyes are moistened by tears,*
> *the hairs on their body will stand on end.*
> *These are the ones who have the seeds of awakened minds.*
> *They are the right recipients of the wisdom of emptiness.*
> *They should be taught the absolute truth.*

Of course, some of these concepts may sound archaic, but they hold the truth. Personally, I've witnessed that some people have a strong resistance to the emptiness teachings, while other people are totally open to them. At one time, I was completely into emptiness and no-self, and would speak about those topics at every event. During a talk I gave at a particular spiritual community, one person in the audience was so moved that she kept crying out of devotion as she heard the topic. Later I met with her and she said that she loved emptiness more than any other subject.

So the scholars say that the monks and nuns indicated in this verse are not just ordinary monks and nuns but are arhats or bodhisattvas who have almost an inborn or karmic affinity with the teachings on emptiness. They have the readiness and courage to hear and understand such a profound truth.

Thus Have I Heard...

When we read this verse, we can imagine that Buddha is residing at Vulture Peak Mountain, surrounded by all the arhats and bodhisattvas, who have big hearts, who have *bodhichitta*, and who have seen the truth, the great emptiness, or who are just dying to hear the teachings on emptiness.

You might like to visualize that whole scene in your mind if you can. You can even think that you are one of those fully ordained monks and nuns, even though technically you are not a monk or nun. Just remember "monks and nuns" refer to the arhats or bodhisattvas who are yearning or longing to hear the teachings on the great emptiness.

The Courageous Ones

In this verse, we come across the word *bodhisattva*. What is a bodhisattva? In Tibetan, *bodhisattva* is *jang chup sem wa* (*byang chub sems dpa'*). Sometimes the Tibetans used the method of meaning translation, and made up totally new Tibetan words for Sanskrit words, with no connection in terms of etymology. The Tibetan translation for *bodhisattva* is one example.

They used the word *jang chup* in Tibetan for *bodhi*, which in general means awakening or enlightenment. In Tibetan etymology, *jang chup* is two words: *jang* and *chup*; *jang* means to purify, and *chup* means realization or actualization. In that sense, *jang chup* is the enlightenment that has two qualities: purification and actualization—the purification of all the inner obscurations, and actualization of all the inner awakened qualities.

Tibetans translated the Sanskrit word *sattva* into *sem wa* (*sems dpa'*), which means the courageous one. It carries the meaning of one who has the courage to practice the bodhisattva's way—to live in the world limitless times and face limitless challenges, in order to help limitless beings—as well as one who has the courage to overcome and conquer the army of Mara, the army of delusion. This is one of the ways to interpret the word *bodhisattva*. Traditionally, bodhisattva means one who holds *bodhichitta*, the awakened heart, the aspiration to become enlightened for the benefit of all beings. Even today, people take the bodhisattva's vow and hold that aspiration.

Bodhisattva may seem like a remote ideal, something that we cannot be. Yet the moment bodhichitta arises in our mind, we become a bodhisattva right then. This is expressed in a verse by Shantideva, who wrote the famous *Bodhicharyavatara*, *The Way of the Bodhisattva*. The verse says,

> *The moment bodhichitta arises,*
> *even those who are bound in the prison of samsara,*
> *will be heirs of the buddhas,*
> *and be worthy to be worshipped by gods and humans.*

Thus Have I Heard...

Buddha's Samadhi

The *Heart Sutra* verse says that Buddha suddenly entered samadhi. But a debate went back and forth between the early panditas and scholars about whether or not Buddha really entered samadhi at that time. Some said Buddha was always residing in samadhi, so he couldn't actually have entered samadhi just then at Vulture Peak Mountain. But that argument was just semantical, so we don't have to pay attention to it now.

It is said that Buddha entered a particular samadhi that we translated as "the samadhi that expresses the Dharma called 'Profound Illumination.'" That's quite an accurate translation. However, the panditas and scholars do not always agree with each other on how to define this particular samadhi. This samadhi actually refers to the samadhi of emptiness. *Profound* refers to the profound truth, which means emptiness; *illumination* refers to understanding, the realization of or awakening to the great emptiness. Basically, the samadhi that Buddha entered is the Buddha's deep meditation on the great emptiness.

The *Heart Sutra* has a very interesting format. In the other *Prajnaparamita Sutras*, Buddha speaks quite often. Yet here Buddha hardly utters any words, except toward the end. It seems he didn't verbally participate in the main topic of emptiness. Rather, Avalokiteshvara answers. Yet this is considered Buddha's sermon. It is almost as if Buddha spoke through Avalokiteshvara. Buddha was obviously meditating on emptiness; here, he is the master of this topic and witness of the dialogue that will soon take place between Avalokiteshvara and Shariputra.

Let's look at the next paragraph.

3

At the same time...

At the same time, noble Avalokiteshvara, the Bodhisattva Mahasattva, while engaging in the profound transcendent wisdom, clearly saw the five skandhas to be empty of nature.

Avalokiteshvara appears quite often in the Mahayana sutras, along with other bodhisattvas, such as Manjushri and Vajrapani. It seems that he was a bodhisattva who was present when Buddha gave the Mahayana teachings and the *Prajnaparamita Sutras*.

Avalokiteshvara is sometimes depicted as the fully awakened Sambhogakaya Buddha, but in the sutras where we find Avalokiteshvara as a disciple of the Buddha, such as here in the *Heart Sutra*, he is regarded as a bodhisattva.

He is also one of the Eight Bodhisattvas in the Mahayana tradition. Even though there are numerous bodhisattvas in the Mahayana tradition, these eight are quite significant. The Eight Bodhisattvas have a big following, almost their own cult in Mahayana. There are even mountains dedicated as sacred abodes to some of them.

We may see different forms of Avalokiteshvara, such as the four-armed Avalokiteshvara, the thousand-armed Avalokiteshvara, and other forms as well. In the Tibetan tradition, Avalokiteshvara often appears as a male bodhisattva. In Chinese Buddhism, Avalokiteshvara appears as Kuan Yin, who is a female bodhisattva. There doesn't seem to be a strong gender identity for Avalokiteshvara in Mahayana Buddhism. Some perceive Avalokiteshvara as a male, while others perceive Avalokiteshvara as a female. Sometimes Avalokiteshvara is androgynous. Ultimately, we can't refer to Avalokiteshvara by gender.

Once when I was visiting a historical city in South Korea, we went to see a very old temple. It was built around the sixth century, though they kept remodeling and renovating it. At one point, we came across a temple building enshrining two images of Avalokiteshvara, or Kuan Yin, right next to each other. One had a mustache, the other didn't. Other than that, there was no difference between them. I asked one of my hosts, "In your tradition, is Avalokiteshvara considered male or female?" And he said, "We are not sure about that. We never figured it out." I said, "Let's leave it like that." It's quite amazing; we have to let go of any kind of gender identity that we might want to superimpose on Avalokiteshvara or Kuan Yin or the ineffable.

Shariputra, an Arhat

In this sutra, Avalokiteshvara is the one answering the questions on emptiness posed by Shariputra. Shariputra, who became an arhat in his lifetime, was a monk, a historical figure, and a student of Buddha Shakyamuni. There are a lot of anecdotes regarding Shariputra in the sutras. He often had many dialogues with Buddha himself.

In the *Heart Sutra*, Shariputra asks Avalokiteshvara vital questions concerning the great emptiness. Yet as we read in the previous verse, Buddha didn't say even one word. He entered the profound samadhi on emptiness and presided as a witness more than anything else.

One may wonder, since Shariputra is already an arhat, why would he bother asking another disciple of Buddha about emptiness? Their dialogue is like a metaphor showing different stages of awakening. It is said that many of the arhats hadn't realized emptiness completely, whereas Avalokiteshvara represents the consciousness fully awakened to emptiness. The dialogue also shows the progress of awakening, since we see that Shariputra wasn't just content with some smaller level of awakening, but was ready for the next level.

Shariputra is a very important disciple of the Buddha. If you look at the iconography of Buddha in Tibetan *thangkas*, you see that Buddha is surrounded by two disciples, Shariputra and Maudgalyayana. Even though Buddha had so many disciples, these two are depicted around Buddha in iconography because they were the two foremost disciples when Buddha was alive.

However, in the Mahayana tradition, Buddha had disciples who were bodhisattvas at a higher level of awakening than those two; Shariputra was not considered a student with the highest awakening in Mahayana. Usually the *shravakas*, such as Shariputra, were considered the lesser of the three categories of practitioners, *shravakas*, *pratyekabuddhas*, and bodhisattvas. On the other hand, some Mahayanists believe that Shariputra and other monks, such as Maudgalyayana and Ananda, were completely enlightened, even though they took the form of listeners, or shravakas. They had big hearts and minds, able to experience emptiness and bodhichitta.

Five Skandhas

The text says that Avalokiteshvara was having a profound realization, seeing the five skandhas to be empty of nature. Here in the *Heart Sutra*, we are establishing emptiness in relationship to the five skandhas, which cover a large domain of all phenomenal reality. The five skandhas are form, feeling, perception, mental formation, and consciousness.

In general, all the Buddhist teachings have two topics: relative truth and ultimate truth. The five skandhas are considered relative truth, while emptiness falls into the topic of ultimate truth. The relative truth and the ultimate truth are interdependent, and one cannot exist without the other. In the end, we cannot even separate them. The integration of the two truths is widely spoken of in Mahayana Buddhist writing. The relative truth categories, such as the five skandhas, are designed to lead us to a deeper understanding of the phenomenal reality, while the ultimate truth leads to seeing the emptiness of all phenomena.

Form

The first of the five skandhas, form, is easy to understand. In Sanskrit, form is *rupa*. It is roughly anything that is tangible, and yet to really understand *rupa* in this context, we may also have to look into Abhidharma.

When you look around, you see the world is mostly form: the chair you are sitting on, the computer you are working on, or even the clouds in the sky are considered form. Big things like mountains and rivers, small things like a pin or a napkin, and sacred things like statues and stupas are all considered form.

In relationship to our own being, we can think of the body as the form. We all have this physical reality—the body, or form—that we identify with. It is not an illusion; this body is real.

Feeling

Feeling, or sensation, is the experience that comes into being when our consciousness, our sense faculty, and an object are in contact with each other. There are five faculties associated with the five senses, and a sixth one associated with the mind consciousness, which is a little more subtle.

For example, after being outside on a cold day, if you come inside and sit next to a fireplace, you'll notice that the feeling or sensation in your body changes. The object in this example is the heat radiating from the fire. The heat is experienced in your consciousness through the body faculty, becoming a sensation of warmth.

There are three kinds of feelings: pleasant, unpleasant, and neutral. We can further divide these feelings into six, related to the six sense faculties: eye, ear, nose, tongue, body, and mind. Thus, we can divide feelings into eighteen categories.

At the Same Time...

Perception, Mental Formations, and Consciousness

Then there is perception, the third skandha. This is easy to understand; it is how we perceive things individually. Perception is not always a consensus; we each can have totally contrasting perceptions of the same reality. There are many categories of perception in Abhidharma.

The fourth skandha is mental formations, or the *samskara* skandha. Not all mental formations are thoughts, though many of them are. There are two kinds of mental formations, and we may need further study of Abhidharma in order to understand them. Basically, the five skandhas are a way of encompassing all compounded reality, and any compounded reality that doesn't belong to the other four skandhas automatically falls into the fourth skandha. Many psychological states come under this umbrella.

The skandha of consciousness is the fifth skandha. Consciousness is a very specific concept in this context. We should not superimpose our casual idea of consciousness on this notion. The definition of consciousness, and how many consciousnesses there are, depend on the school of thought; there may be six or eight consciousnesses.

Let me not give a long commentary right now on the ending phrase, "clearly saw the five skandhas to be *empty of nature*." As time goes by, we'll learn what "empty of nature" means from the point of view of the *Prajnaparamita Sutras*.

4

The Path of the Bodhisattvas

Before we get into the heart of this sutra, which is a complete teaching on emptiness, let's talk a bit more about some basic Mahayana Buddhist themes and concepts, such as the bodhisattva and bodhichitta.

Mahayana Buddhism is a tradition and path that is closely associated with the way of the bodhisattvas. Mahayana itself developed as a tradition in early Buddhist history in India and flourished in various regions in Asia. It extended toward Central and Far East Asia and also reached Southeast Asia, where it later became extinct. Today it is the Buddhism that people practice in countries such as Tibet, Bhutan, China, Mongolia, and Japan. Sometimes we also refer to the schools of the Mahayana doctrine, which are usually divided into the Chittamatra and Madhyamaka schools.

The Lotus of Mahayana

Let's look at the etymology of the word *Mahayana*: *maha* means great in Sanskrit, and *yana* means vehicle. In that sense, Mahayana is like the great vehicle that carries one to enlightenment. The idea is that Mahayana is altruistic and noble because it is a path in which one does not seek enlightenment for one's own benefit; one wants to dedicate one's own effort to awaken all other beings to nirvana, absolute freedom.

In the classical texts, it is said that Mahayana has seven great qualities that distinguish it from other traditions. These qualities, which are explained in the *Mahayana Sutralamkara Karika* by Acharya Asanga, are:

1. Great object of focus
2. Great practice
3. Great wisdom
4. Great diligence
5. Great skill in means
6. Great perfect accomplishment
7. Great enlightened activity

There are quite extensive explanations on these seven points in the traditional texts. But there are a few main, important characteristics that make Mahayana what it is. It emphasizes boundless compassion toward all beings and also teaches the doctrine of emptiness. It holds the idea that one does not escape from samsara or the world but engages with it, and practices the way of the bodhisattva in order to help others.

If one were to use a simile or metaphor to describe Mahayana, it would be a lotus. Of course, Mahayana does not have ownership of that metaphor because a lotus is often used in Buddhism as well as in other traditions. And yet it can be used with Mahayana, depending on its interpretation. Tibetan Mahayana Buddhists often use a simile of the lotus to describe the highest awakening. For example, the fifteenth-century Mahamudra master Shamara Khachod Wangpo wrote in one of his songs of realization,

> *It hasn't been dried by the sunlight of nirvana;*
> *It hasn't been polluted by the mud of samsara.*
> *It does not depend on either but it is not separate from either.*
> *I, the yogi, am like this lotus.*

I don't know exactly what the author's intent is, but this is a beautiful and interesting verse, and we can give our own interpretation. The first line says the lotus hasn't dried up. Sometimes when spiritual people become so entrenched in transcendence, they tend to lose the juiciness of life, lose their passion, and become lost in the idea of nirvana. Their natural flow of life can be constrained by their grand concepts. Also, stating that the lotus is not polluted by mud is a popular interpretation of Mahayana practice, where you stay in the world but are not bound by the delusions of the world. This is one way of describing Mahayana.

The Heroic Ones

The *Prajnaparamita Sutras* are ultimately teachings about the path of the bodhisattva. We can't really separate the Prajnaparamita teachings from the bodhisattva's path. That's why it will be very helpful to spend a little bit of time to understand more about the characteristics of the bodhisattva.

There are many ways of explaining the meaning of bodhisattva. One of the easiest ways to explain bodhisattva and the path is by reciting a verse from Shantideva's text, the *Bodhicharyavatara, The Way of the Bodhisattva*. Most people are familiar with this text. It has been translated into English in a number of different versions. There is one verse that people often quote from that text:

For as long as space remains,
for as long as sentient beings remain,
until then, may I too remain
to dispel the miseries of the world.

This verse is a perfect description of a bodhisattva's vow. You are making an almost eternal commitment to help others, to live altruistically. You can see that one's wish to live in this world forever and to help others requires an unbelievable level of courage.

As we said earlier, *bodhisattva* means the awakened heroine or hero who has a great heart and courage. A bodhisattva is somebody who is not seeking peace or nirvana for herself but has a big heart that can embrace all living beings, all creatures that exist in this world, and who is willing to be in samsara, the world of sorrow. This is why bodhisattvas are considered the heroic and courageous ones. They are willing to remain in the world, in samsara, forever, as long as sentient beings remain, to be with them and to be sympathetic with their sorrow. A bodhisattva won't just go away from the world to enjoy her own nirvana, her own peace, but has a heartfelt commitment, a vow, to stay in the world to dispel the miseries of this world. This turns out to be very courageous.

The Awakened Heart

Enlightenment or nirvana is not always interpreted the same, since each tradition has its own way of describing it. And yet they all agree it is the ultimate liberation.

Historically, it seems that many monks and nuns were seeking nirvana for themselves. They felt that this world was a place of unending sorrow. Their whole aspiration, their whole goal of walking the spiritual path, was to get away from this world as soon as possible. They saw the world as a world of impurity and sorrow, so they entered the spiritual path in order to experience a total extinction of human suffering and to become almost nonexistent. That was their desire.

However, the Mahayana Buddhists felt that this kind of desire or aspiration was limited and finite. Mahayana Buddhists taught that the spiritual path motivated by such limited desire could not actually lead anyone to complete perfect awakening. So they started teaching and practicing bodhichitta, the awakened heart, almost as an antidote to such a limited aspiration. Bodhichitta is a powerful aspiration to awaken to the ultimate in order to benefit all sentient beings in the universe.

So the bodhisattvas are courageous because they have a big heart and a vow to remain in the world forever, as long as sentient beings remain. You can see that this is actually a kind of unthinkable courage. We are not seeking liberation for ourselves, but we are vowing to remain in this world as long as space remains, as long as sentient beings remain. We are vowing to be with them, to be open hearted, to be sympathetic with their miseries, and to help them.

Now, we have to realize this is not always logical. We cannot even say that we can be in this world forever, to be with all sentient beings, until samsara is empty. Maybe this is not even possible; we don't know. Samsara may never be empty.

There is a legend that tells how unthinkable and profound such courage can be, and shows that it is not easy to maintain such courage in the face of challenges. Once, the legend says, Avalokiteshvara made a very strong commitment never to give up bodhichitta and to continuously bring all beings to absolute liberation. In his mind, he thought he had helped all the beings in the universe to find inner peace, to find freedom from samsara. But as he returned to his paradise, Potala, he looked back and saw that the world of samsara hadn't changed at all. There were still an infinite number of beings lost and confused and tormented. Seeing this, he became exhausted, and wanted to give up his commitment, his hope; he just wanted to find peace for himself. Because of the power of his bodhichitta aspiration, the moment he had the thought of giving up, his head fell into ten pieces and his body fell into a thousand pieces.

At that moment, Buddha Amitabha showed up and touched Avalokiteshvara's broken body with his hand, blessing him and transforming him into the eleven-headed Avalokiteshvara with a thousand arms. Then Avalokiteshvara rose again, in order to continuously help others. This legend shows the profound courage of bodhichitta and also shows it is not easy, because the suffering of the world is overwhelming.

In Shantideva's verse that we quoted earlier, the bodhisattva is praying that she will not only remain in this world forever but will keep dispelling the sorrow of this world. Is this even possible? Is it really possible that we can remain in the world forever and keep dispelling the sorrow of the world?

A Transcendent Aspiration

There are three kinds of *bodhichitta*, or the bodhisattva's aspiration: the king-like bodhichitta, the captain-like bodhichitta, and the herder-like bodhichitta. In the king-like bodhichitta, you hold the aspiration that you will become enlightened first and then you'll awaken all beings. The captain-like bodhichitta is the bodhisattva's aspiration to become enlightened together with all living beings. And in the herder-like bodhichitta, you vow to awaken all sentient beings and you stay behind after everyone becomes enlightened, and then you let yourself become enlightened.

Now the question is, are these aspirations rational or logical in the first place? Can we awaken anybody? Can we awaken all living beings? Is it really possible that we can awaken all living beings?

Years ago, I was giving a discourse on bodhichitta, and somebody raised her hand and said, "This notion of bodhichitta is very inspiring, but it's not logical. How can you liberate everyone? That is impossible." I said, "Absolutely, you are right. It is impossible for you or me to liberate all living beings. That is not our task." So bodhichitta is not logical or rational; rather, it is a deep aspiration, a transcendent aspiration. This aspiration never arises from the mind, but rather from the heart. Bodhichitta is the unflinching longing to be awakened to the absolute as soon as possible, not for oneself but for all living beings.

The point is that bodhichitta, which may not be logical or rational, is an aspiration that we can hold in order to open our own heart, to make our mind and heart much bigger. In the end, bodhichitta is about our own inner development. It is all about widening and expanding our own heart and becoming more selfless and courageous. It is not about whether or not in reality we can awaken all living beings in this existence. Bodhichitta is the aspiration to help others, to help humanity, to be the source of positive influence, and to make a spiritual contribution—a contribution of love and wisdom—to this human world. That is the mission of a bodhisattva.

The Bodhisattva's Practices

The bodhisattva has a complete path, and the six *paramitas* are what we can call the spiritual observances of the bodhisattvas. The six paramitas are generosity, discipline, tolerance (or courage or patience), diligence, meditation, and transcendent wisdom. *Prajnaparamita,* or transcendent wisdom, is the nonconceptual understanding of the absolute.

Shantideva often said that of the six paramitas, the last one is the most important. He even said that the last one was like the queen or king, and the first five were like the retinue or entourage of this great queen or king. In that sense, Mahayana Buddhists tend to teach that the one thing that leads us to inner awakening is wisdom, *Prajnaparamita.* If that is missing, then an important ingredient is missing. In a famous statement, one of the great ancient masters, Dharmakirti, said,

> *Virtues such as compassion and love*
> *are not in direct opposition to ignorance*
> *so they will not cut through the root of samsara, ignorance.*

In other words, he said that without wisdom, you can never be free, even though you may practice the path of compassion and love. He said love and compassion alone cannot set you free; you need wisdom.

What he is saying is that it is very possible that we can be very spiritual—practicing love and compassion, going around doing good things for humanity—and still be lost and deluded if we don't have wisdom. The other observances or practices, such as generosity and discipline, can assist us in going through all the different stages of awakening along the path, but wisdom is the very element that can wake us up. Indeed, wisdom itself is awakening.

In summary, there are six paramitas, the six practices of the bodhisattvas. The sixth one, transcendent wisdom, is the most important one because that is the very thing that awakens us. The *Prajnaparamita Sutras*, such as the *Heart Sutra*, deal with the last paramita—transcendent wisdom, *prajnaparamita*.

Let's continue to the next paragraph in the *Heart Sutra*.

5

Then, through the inspiration...

> *Then, through the inspiration of the Buddha, venerable Shariputra said to noble Avalokiteshvara, the Bodhisattva Mahasattva, "How should a son or daughter of noble family train, who wishes to follow the profound path of transcendent wisdom?"*

Here it is saying that Shariputra was in some way inspired or motivated to engage in this profound dialogue with Avalokiteshvara. He asked Avalokiteshvara how sons and daughters of noble family should engage with the profound truth, the great emptiness.

The words "sons and daughters of noble family" refer to those individuals with a big heart, or those who have the mental capacity, courage, as well as a karmic affinity to hear the *Prajnaparamita Sutras* or teachings on emptiness. So it does not refer to just any of Buddha's disciples, because some of Buddha's disciples were not ready to hear the teachings on emptiness.

There are a lot of stories that say many of Buddha's disciples became scared and intimidated the moment they heard the Buddha's teachings on the great emptiness. They could not tolerate the Prajnaparamita teachings. This happened not only during Buddha's time, but continued through generations that came later. The effect of this reaction is often reflected in the works of the early Mahayana Buddhist masters, such as Nagarjuna, who had to defend the Prajnaparamita teachings. It was not just a few individuals who couldn't understand emptiness; there was almost an entire movement that philosophically resisted the Mahayana sutras, especially the idea of great emptiness.

So when we read the words, "sons and daughters of noble family," *noble family* does not mean they come from an important, rich, or aristocratic family. It refers to those who belong to the Mahayana family and have the courage to hear the *Prajnaparamita Sutras*, the teachings on the profound emptiness.

The ideal bodhisattva is not only someone who has the willingness to stay in samsara and awaken all beings, but also has the mental capacity to contemplate mahashunyata, the great emptiness, which turns out to be a very profound but also quite frightening truth for many people. Such bodhisattvas have the true courage to be awakened to the great emptiness, which is sometimes beyond the comprehension of a small mind or small heart.

The Frightening Dimension of Emptiness

Why is it said that emptiness can be frightening and intimidating to some people? We might like to explore that frightening dimension of the teachings on the great emptiness.

It is said that in the beginning Buddha didn't really teach what he had discovered—the great emptiness. We know that at first, Buddha didn't want to teach. He made a very famous statement when he became enlightened:

> *I have found a teaching like ambrosia, profound, peaceful,*
> *free from conception, luminous, uncreated.*
> *If I tell of this teaching, no one will understand.*
> *So I shall stay in the forest without speaking.*

Finally two celestial beings encouraged Buddha to teach. Buddha was a skillful master and often taught in accordance with what his audience could handle. Therefore, he often taught a simple Dharma, a simple spirituality. He taught a basic, exoteric spirituality based on ethical guidelines, a path that could lead to earthly happiness and well-being. Buddha clearly taught in a way that his audience could relate to. For example, he gave advice to the kings on how to govern the country, and to lay people on how to be a better spouse. It is said that now and then in his sermons, Buddha even declared there is a personal self.

In the end, Buddha did everything in his power to lead people to awakening—awakening to the profound truth—so he also taught what might have been shocking to the minds of the masses, such as when he negated a personal self. When Buddha negated the personal self, that teaching became known as *anatman* (Sanskrit), or *anatta* (Pali). It was a shocking truth for many people.

Eventually, it seems many early Buddhists accepted *anatta*, emptiness of a personal self. Yet even though they accepted *anatta*, or emptiness of a personal self, some early Buddhists couldn't really accept the idea that somehow everything else is also empty. Mahashunyata is not just negating the personal self but also negating the inherent reality of everything that exists, including buddhahood, enlightenment, nirvana, and samsara. That was a shocking teaching and truth for many people—the idea that everything was not as real as they thought. This is why emptiness can be very frightening, so frightening that it is said that some monks died right there on the spot when they heard the teachings on emptiness for the first time.

Maybe this is why Buddha offered guidance about who was allowed to hear the *Prajnaparamita Sutras* and the

Mahayana teachings in general. He came up with a kind of logic or analysis that could tell a person's mental and spiritual capacity, and whether he or she was ready to hear the Mahayana teachings. This analysis is taught in the Mahayana sutra called *Chö Chu Pé Do* (*chos bcu pa'i mdo*), the *Sutra on Ten Dharmas*:

> *One knows there is fire because there is smoke;*
> *that there is water because of the bird;*
> *In the same way, you'll know the bodhisattvas by the signs they demonstrate.*
> *The nature of these wise bodhisattvas can be known.*

So emptiness can be very frightening. I often use an old Chinese parable to explain this. One time there was an artist in ancient China who was in love with the dragon. He painted his whole house with the image of a dragon, and he painted his whole body with the image of a dragon. The dragon in the sky finally heard the rumor that there was a very crazy artist who was totally in love with the dragon. The dragon was a little flattered and decided to visit the artist.

One day, the dragon came down from heaven and arrived at the artist's house. And as dragons do, instead of going through the door, he entered through the window. The artist was busy painting a dragon, and suddenly he saw at the window, not the dragon that he was in love with, but a monstrous creature that was going to eat him at any moment. He ran away and fainted.

I use this parable to describe the frightening dimension of emptiness. The whole idea that everything is empty of true existence, or inherent reality, is very frightening for many people's ego to hear.

Mahayana Buddhists recite all the *Prajnaparamita Sutras* and literally worship the great emptiness. Emptiness is the foundation of the Mahayana Buddhist path and Tantric Buddhism, too. For example, when Tantric Buddhists practice the sadhanas in Vajrayana, they are reminded again and again that the deities in Tantric Buddhism are just expressions of the great emptiness. They symbolize emptiness. So emptiness is the life force, the heart, the soul, not just of Zen Buddhism or Mahayana but of Tantric Buddhism, too.

At the same time, if we actually experience emptiness, then we may not like it, just as the crazy artist didn't like the dragon. He just liked the idea, the concept, of a dragon. But he really didn't love the dragon when he saw it. He found it to be a very intimidating, scary, monstrous creature. In the same way, even if you love and worship the idea of emptiness, if you begin to experience emptiness, then you may not like it. You may actually resist it.

Then, through the inspiration...

Nonconceptual Emptiness

As the rational mind focuses in, we always want to put everything into a box or compartmentalize it. This is even true for our quest to understand emptiness. In some sense, every intellectual understanding of emptiness is incomplete in itself until you have a direct experience of it. This is why it is so necessary to remind ourselves that we should not hook into or be attached to our own intellectual understanding of emptiness. Our intellectual understanding of emptiness is not really what emptiness is.

This is also why Buddhists argue with each other about how to define emptiness. They are arguing about their intellectual understanding. They are arguing about a mental construct that only exists in their heads. If it was not a mental construct but instead some *thing* we could all agree on, there would be no debate about it.

So emptiness is not some kind of theory that we have to keep refining in order to get to the most accurate and valid theory, or in order to say, "Now I understand emptiness because I've been investigating it and refining what emptiness is. Now I understand emptiness, and I just need to meditate on it."

This is not what true emptiness is. This is not how we are supposed to meditate on emptiness. But somehow even some great Tibetan thinkers fall into the trap of thinking that if you keep analyzing, investigating, and trying to understand emptiness by comparing all the various doctrines, using your own intelligence, and reading all the ancient scriptures, eventually you will arrive at a point where you feel you have an accurate, valid, conceptual understanding of emptiness. Then you can just meditate on it. But you see this is still completely mental and conceptual.

Emptiness is not something we can understand through the intellect or the thinking mind. We have to go beyond the realm of the thinking mind to truly have the direct realization of it. There is emptiness in each of us. Emptiness here means empty of all concepts, empty of all struggles, empty of all duality, and empty of all notions of self—empty of all your ideas of who you are. Empty of your past and future, empty of birth and death, empty of duality between enemy and friends... empty of everything. It is the true nature of reality.

The Tibetan Buddhists of the Nyingma, Sakya, and Gelug traditions have been debating, writing refutations, and accusing each other, saying the others' understanding of emptiness is wrong. The Nyingmapas said, "We understand what true emptiness is," and they said Gelugpas and Sakyapas didn't really understand emptiness very well. And of course, all the Gelugpas, practitioners of Gelug, wrote refutations, accusing the other schools of not having the right understanding of emptiness. This actually shows that the emptiness that many people think about and worship is just a mental construct, a theory. I hope this is making sense.

So to me, emptiness is not a theory. Ultimately, it is not something we can understand. It is an internal experience. It is a powerful process of letting go and dropping all our illusions, all the illusions that we are holding on to.

I think one tricky aspect of all these teachings is that we can turn them into some kind of philosophy. It can, of course, be a very wonderful and profound philosophy. Some of these philosophies can be really misleading, too. And now people are also mixing the idea of great emptiness with quantum physics, which is very questionable. It can lead people to think that emptiness means that nothing is physically present, which can be nihilistic.

There is a trend that began in the early twentieth century of establishing a marriage between science and Buddhism, because science in the Western mind (and now in the Eastern mind, too) was almost an unquestionable religion. There is nothing wrong with science. Science is a great adventure for exploring the nature of reality, and it has done countless good things for humanity. There is no doubt that there are areas where Buddhism and science meet each other. But it can also be dangerous to try to fit Buddhism completely into a scientific paradigm; we may destroy something very precious. In the end, emptiness is a profound spiritual and subjective experience of letting go of our clinging to the illusions we construct. This does not need to be validated by science.

Flavors of Awakening

As we said, in some early Buddhist traditions, *anatta* was taught but that was as far as they went. Some early Buddhists negated the personal self, but they didn't really get into the emptiness of everything or the idea that everything is illusory. Everything that exists is empty, including the things we regard as sacred—nirvana, buddhahood, and so forth. Buddha himself is empty, too.

In the end, it seems this whole meditation or contemplation on emptiness is an inner process of awakening, particularly a process of letting go.

I feel that the process of awakening has two flavors: one is letting go and one is more like flourishing and blossoming. When I say flourishing and blossoming, I mean that you feel like you are arriving at a spiritual insight. You feel that your heart is blossoming; you feel that your love, your joy, your true freedom are blossoming and flourishing. You feel that you are thriving inside in a very non-egoic way.

The other flavor of awakening is letting go. You feel you are letting go, you are dissolving. You are letting go of your attachment; you are letting go of your illusions. The process of letting go can be liberating, but it can sometimes be challenging, too, as if a rug has been pulled out from under you. It can feel like we are directly destroying the world we know, the world that we have been living in. It is like a huge paradigm shift in our understanding of what reality is. This is not always an easy process to digest.

I hope you understand what I am trying to say. Awakening has two flavors: one is letting go and the other one is like blossoming. Awakening can be inspiring; it can be beautiful as well as ecstatic, too.

Letting Go

So in the beginning, emptiness is negation, and in the end, it is not negation. The great Indian master Aryadeva said that in the beginning you negate the unwholesome, in the middle you negate the personal self, and in the end you go beyond everything, which means you don't negate anything. So in the end, maybe emptiness is not negation. Maybe it's just a complete ecstatic awakening in which all the chains in your psyche are broken, and you feel in harmony with totality.

Yet on the path, when we start meditating on emptiness, it is definitely a process of negating, because it involves letting go. We have to go through that process of letting go; we have to let go of something in order to be free, to be liberated inside. Not rejecting but letting go, burning.

What do we have to let go of? Ultimately, we are supposed to let go of everything for a while. We let go of everything we are attached to and deconstruct all of our illusions. This is why emptiness is a negation, even though sometimes our ego doesn't like negation because it seems to be very painful or inconvenient. Sometimes our ego just loves to go through the process of accumulation. Accumulation in Buddhism is the idea that one is acquiring everything wholesome—the wholesome Dharma, the wholesome path, faith, wisdom, compassion, generosity. They are all good and can be conducive factors for one's awakening, yet they can be limited when the practice of letting go is lacking.

It seems that when some people enter the Buddhist path, they never go through a process of letting go. They go through a process of acquiring observances, getting all these wonderful things—all the belief systems and beautiful illusions. They get enamored with the beautiful language and all the beautiful practices. They keep all their neuroses as well as the usual illusions that everyone is attached to, and then they add countless illusions and belief systems to their minds: illusions about the guru as a personal savior, the path, enlightenment, and so forth, which have nothing to do with the actual guru, path, and enlightenment. I'm not saying there is anything wrong with all these acquisitions. But we have so many illusions around these notions, and the illusions have to be deconstructed in order to understand the true meaning and purpose of all the notions we find in Buddhism or in other traditions, too.

Even in the Buddhist tradition, we find so many people fall prey to illusions, which either they create themselves or their community collectively constructs. As an example, one of the big illusions is the illusion of the guru. People often take somebody as a guru and see this person as some kind of perfect and magical person. They take him as a personal savior, thinking they don't have to do anything. They don't have to do inquiry, or develop love or compassion. They think, "As long as we worship the guru, our souls are going to be saved." This kind of illusion can be detrimental to one's personal growth and spiritual development. It's a form of letting go of responsibility for one's own awakening. It almost contradicts what Buddha said: "I can only show you the path; you must walk it." Please don't misunderstand—this is not to say we don't need a guru. A guru is a very important factor in our individual path to awakening. However, the role of a guru is not to save us but to guide us and to show us our own innate wisdom and strength.

I don't see that there is a way to enlightenment as far as Buddhism is concerned without going through the process of emptiness, which is a process of letting go. Without the process of letting go, our path is incomplete because we will never be able to deconstruct the illusions that bind us. Without going through the process of emptiness, we cannot be liberated at the root.

Three Stages on the Path

There are different stages of the spiritual path; obviously, the first stage is working with the basic spiritual principles, such as compassion and ethics, including the practices of nonviolence and generosity. Yet that is not the whole endeavor. We can also engage with more profound contemplations that can remove the veils of limiting concepts and perceptions in our psyche, in order to see the nature of reality from another perspective.

Aryadeva, who was a student of the great master Nagarjuna, laid out a map that shows three major stages on the path to awakening. There are many stages, but he synthesized them into three, which we briefly quoted earlier.

The first is to negate all the unwholesome. The second is to negate the personal self. The third, he said, goes beyond all the doctrines, or *ta wa* (lta ba). *Ta wa* means philosophical views. Aryadeva said,

> At first, turn away from non-virtue;
> In the middle, dispel misconceptions of self.
> Finally, go beyond all philosophical views.
> One who understands this is wise indeed.

Basically, Aryadeva said that when people enter the spiritual path, one of the first things they need to do is abandon what is unwholesome, such as violence. Violence is action we engage in that harms living beings, action that is caused by intentions such as hatred. To refrain from violence is the ground of all spiritual development in almost every tradition. Nonviolence is like a golden rule affirmed by all the sacred traditions.

Then Aryadeva talked about the second stage on the path to enlightenment. He said, "In the middle, dispel misconceptions of self." And in the end, the final stage, you go beyond all philosophical assertions, including existence, nonexistence, emptiness, and so forth.

Is this whole process of negation important on the path to the great awakening? It is important because we can see that the root cause of our delusion—the samsara that we are trying to wake up from—is actually the whole world of concepts, beliefs, and illusions that we are attached to. That's why we may have to go through this stage of deconstructing and letting go, emptying or negating something, whatever that might be—the personal self, illusions, concepts, and so forth.

Negation in Other Traditions

Negation is part of many spiritual traditions. In Christianity, negation is very important. They say there are two ways of understanding God. One method is through affirmation, meditating on what God is. Another way, used in the contemplative Christian tradition, is meditating on what God is not. Christians call this the *via negativa*, which is a process of deconstructing your concepts, ideas, and illusions through inquiry. It is a way to realize that the divine is ineffable. They say you can never understand what God is; even God doesn't understand himself. God is a transcendent being. So the *via negativa* is a powerful, radical contemplative practice to arrive at the perfect understanding of God by negating, rather than affirming, what God is.

Some Christian mystics also taught a negation-based inquiry. Meister Eckhart, a German mystic, taught a meditation method that has this element of negation. He was often misunderstood when he was alive. His teachings were considered very radical, even controversial.

I heard about understanding God through *via negativa* from a Christian monk many years ago. One time we had a gathering in Napa Valley. A family invited two Christian monks and a Tibetan lama who had never been to the West before and had never met with any Christians. When the lama was informed that the two Christian monks were going to attend the dinner, he was very excited. He said he was going to argue with them to disprove the existence of God and the creator. Usually people have an expectation that theistic traditions believe that God is almost superhuman, with very precise characteristics.

Personally, I was worried that there would be a long debate, and I had no idea how it would turn out. I just wanted to enjoy my dinner. When they sat down together, the Tibetan lama, through the interpreter, asked the older monk, "What is God?" The Christian monk said, "You cannot describe God. God is all-pervasive, beyond words and concepts." The lama didn't initiate an argument with the monk because the monk didn't give a solid concept about God. Thanks to the universe, there was no debate; I was quite relieved. Yet I'm still wondering, if someone asked that monk if God was the creator, would he say yes?

Advaita Vedanta also has negation: the *neti, neti* approach, "not this, not that." The *neti, neti* form of negation is very important for all spiritual development. Without going through the process of negation, we may never be able to deconstruct and let go of our illusions. We may never be able to let go of our concepts and ideas, or our notions of the divine or ineffable. That's why meditation on emptiness is a powerful path to the great awakening.

Shunyata

Some people say we should not translate *shunyata* as emptiness. They say we should use another word, such as openness or fullness. But that is an inaccurate translation in all ways. It ignores the etymology of the word and denies the importance of negating. We have to be very cautious when we translate these extremely important terms based upon our sentiments, feelings, and preferences.

When King Trisong Detsen sponsored the building of the Samye monastery in Tibet in the eighth century, he dedicated one section of that monastery for translation projects, bringing Buddhist texts from Sanskrit into Tibetan. Often the Indian panditas and Tibetan translators worked together, and later the Tibetan king officially sanctioned some of the terms they came up with, so that people couldn't translate them in any way they wanted. He did this because the translators knew that even one important concept can destroy the whole system if it is misunderstood. Of course, in general, it's not usually a good idea for a government to dictate our spiritual practices or translations; that can perhaps block creativity and genius. But on the other hand, it's nice to have some consensus on how we translate some of these important terms.

If you translate *shunyata* as openness instead of emptiness, then there is no negation. I'm sure our ego loves that. We don't have to let go of anything. Ego will say, "This is a good deal. I don't have to let go of anything. The last thing I want to do is let go. It is the least entertaining thing for me to do." So it's very good news for the ego if we can enter the path, we can be enlightened, and we don't have to let go of anything. That's why it is very tricky when we try to translate *shunyata* as openness. Such translation demonstrates that we really don't understand emptiness as a process of negation, an important method, a *neti, neti* method, "not this, not that." Openness can eventually happen, but only after we go through emptiness as a negation.

Deconstructing Illusions

So this approach, this method of deconstruction or letting go, may be an important part of all the contemplative traditions, whether in Buddhism, Vedanta, or Christianity. Logically, it makes sense because we see that our suffering and problems come from believing in our concepts too much. We are all very attached to our own illusions, yet it is hard for us to see them.

I don't think we have to be a meditator or contemplative to see the illusions held by other people. Often in everyday life, it is easy for us to see the falsehood of the concepts, opinions, and belief systems held by others. We see their illusions, but we have a hard time seeing our own illusions; we have difficulty seeing the falsehood of our own concepts and ideas.

Illusion here means a false reality created out of delusion. That's really what illusion is. We can see many people in this world create their own illusions, get lost and caught up in their illusions, and then cause a lot of problems. Maybe this is why the meditation of negation is very important—so we can see through the falsehood of our own illusions and not grasp at them as being so real and so true.

Perhaps this is why there is so much emphasis on negation in the Buddhist tradition, which begins with negating the most cherished illusion we have—the personal self. Then Mahayana Buddhism expands the whole scope of negation to include absolutely everything. It encourages us to investigate everything. In the end, we have to deconstruct all the illusions in our mind, which may require us to say goodbye to all our notions of reality.

Devotion

It seems that we need some kind of love—love for awakening, a burning desire for the ultimate awakening, the desire to wake up from illusions. This is why the sutras and shastras describe those who have the ability to be awakened as having incredible love for the emptiness teachings.

One means for cultivating such devotion is by practicing certain sadhanas, such as the sadhanas based on *Yum Chen Mo*, the Great Mother archetype. The central focus in these sadhanas is the visualization of Yum Chen Mo, the Mother of all the Buddhas, who is a symbol of

Then, through the inspiration...

emptiness. The Great Mother can appear in different forms; sometimes she has two arms, sometimes she has four arms. In the Tibetan tradition, Yum Chen Mo, the Great Mother with Four Arms, is quite popular. This female figure symbolizes the wisdom of the Prajnaparamita.

Nagarjuna himself wrote a sadhana on the Prajnaparamita in which Yum Chen Mo is the focus of the visualization. I feel perhaps Nagarjuna composed this sadhana so we could experience more devotion, longing, and love in relationship to Prajnaparamita and the whole teaching on emptiness.

The reason they use not only a female figure but a mother figure to symbolize Prajnaparamita, or transcendent wisdom, is that all the buddhas are born from this wisdom. The transcendent wisdom, Prajnaparamita, is like the spiritual mother who gives birth to all the arhats, all the sublime bodhisattvas, as well as *samyak-sambuddhas*. As we said earlier, there is the notion in the Mahayana tradition that you cannot experience authentic awakening unless you have gained transcendent wisdom, Prajnaparamita.

The application of the Yum Chen Mo archetype can be a very powerful means to inspire devotion in us. Sometimes it's easier for human beings to experience love, devotion, and heart opening when we can associate those feelings with sacred images and archetypes. It's hard to feel love or devotion when there is no image. It's hard to feel love for emptiness because emptiness is not a thing; it has no image. When you have the longing for emptiness, it can expedite both the process of realizing emptiness as well as the process of letting go. By bringing this element of ecstatic devotion, the Prajnaparamita sadhanas are somewhat of a link between Sutrayana and Vajrayana.

Maybe people also realized that just studying the texts and shastras has a limitation. Some people believe that you don't really have to study too hard, all you need is a lot of longing for and devotion to the great awakening, awakening to emptiness. Then you can just meditate and chant the *Heart Sutra*. With devotion, such practice has the power to lead you to awakening.

This idea that you don't have to study caused a division between two approaches in Buddhism. One approach says you don't have to study scriptures, you just emphasize meditation and then you'll have a profound awakening. Other schools say you have to study the sutras and shastras thoroughly until you gain an accurate intellectual understanding of emptiness, and then you can meditate and be awakened. These two approaches exist in Tibetan Buddhism as well as in other Mahayana traditions, and sometimes they tend to point out each other's shortcomings. These approaches were highlighted around the time of Lama Tsongkhapa, a great teacher of the fourteenth century and the founder of the largest Tibetan Buddhist sect, the Gelug, or the Yellow Hat sect. His followers directly or indirectly criticized the yogis of some traditions for lacking in study and scriptural knowledge. Sometimes they were very blatant in their writings. On the other hand, many Nyingma masters were worried about overemphasizing the study of scriptures, which can be a hinderance to one's meditation practice. Someone could get lost in theories, and never bring the teachings into their experience.

The truth is that we don't have to study scriptures for years to have a profound epiphany. At the same time, studying the Mahayana sutras and shastras can be beneficial and helpful for our inner awakening. In the end, it's good to have a balance between meditation and study, remembering that we can never substitute intellectual knowledge for direct experience.

That being said, the masters of the past always warned that we could easily mistake some "fuzzy" experience, where we no longer feel contracted, for the authentic awakening to emptiness. Those experiences are valuable, but they could be lacking in the true nonconceptual understanding of emptiness. Some of those beautiful experiences could easily fall under the category of *nyam* (*nyams*).

Nyam is one of the three developmental stages of the meditation practice, which include intellectual understanding, *go wa* (*go ba*); meditative experience, *nyam* (*nyams*); and *tokpa* (*rtogs pa*), realization. These stages are all connected with each other; none of them are irrelevant to meditation practices. As developmental stages, none are sufficient by themselves but together, they serve as the way to the realization, the actual authentic awakening. Dzogchen master Prahevajra said,

> *Intellectual understanding is like a patch on clothes.*
> *It will fall off eventually.*
> *Meditative experiences are like mist.*
> *They will dissolve.*
> *Realization is like Mount Meru, unshakable.*
> *It will not perish.*

This verse is saying that both intellectual understanding and meditative experiences are not the real thing in the end; they both have limitations. We should not be content with intellectual understanding only, thinking it is the whole spiritual path. That would be a pitfall. In the same way, nyam can be powerful and transformative but they also have limitations, especially when they are lacking in authentic insight. So now and then, it is important to inquire into one's spiritual experiences to make sure they have depth.

6

Madhyamaka Inquiry

Inquiry is another method of negation. But before we look at inquiry, we need to bring in another topic: Madhyamaka, a philosophical system of logic and reasoning as a meditative inquiry to realize the great emptiness. Madhyamaka is a school of thought with very rich teachings on emptiness.

Buddha did deep inquiry into the very depth of our existence, the human existence as well as the entire existence, and he had a profound breakthrough, which his followers later called Madhyamaka. It literally means the middle view. Here, middle view means wisdom that does not fall into eternalism or nihilism, but stands between them. Buddha taught that as long as we are holding onto either extreme, we are stuck. Madhyamaka is another way of describing the wisdom of emptiness that goes beyond eternalism and nihilism.

Beyond Eternalism and Nihilism

Eternalism is a limited view, and nihilism is a limited view. With both of these mistaken world views, or views of reality, there is always delusion one way or another. With eternalism, usually you are adding something to reality that is not there. There are many examples of eternalism. With nihilism, it is as if you are subtracting or rejecting something from reality. There are many examples of nihilism, and there are also gross and subtle levels of both eternalism and nihilism.

So beyond eternalism and nihilism, there is Madhyamaka, the middle view, which actually reveals reality. It is not a doctrine but the brilliant enlightened mind transcending both eternalism and nihilism.

It is important not to think that the middle view is another philosophical position that we hold onto as a replacement for eternalism or nihilism. The middle view is not something we can be attached to. *Middle view* is just an expression to describe going beyond eternalism and nihilism, but is not a particular place where we can reside. This is why it is said in the *Samadhi Raja Sutra*,

Pure and impure are conceptual extremes.
Compounded and uncompounded are conceptual extremes.
Because of that, the intelligent ones let go of
all conceptual extremes.
They do not even reside in the middle.

Yet not all scholars agree that the middle view is not a philosophical position. Even the verse we quoted is not always interpreted literally. For example, the scholars from the Gelug tradition might not agree that that there is no concrete philosophical position of *middle view*. They often reinterpret this verse. Jamyang Zhépa, a great Gelugpa scholar born in the seventeenth century, said that such a verse is not negating the middle view itself but negating the middle view established by other schools of thought, such as the Chittamatra, who couldn't comprehend the ultimate truth.

Madhyamaka Texts

Nagarjuna and his followers, such as Aryadeva, Chandrakirti, and Shantideva, wrote many texts that focused particularly on emptiness, which Buddha had taught earlier. We call their whole genre of teachings *Madhyamaka*. But Madhyamaka is not different from the Prajnaparamita teachings. It is just another way of describing the wisdom of emptiness that goes beyond eternalism and nihilism.

In the Tibetan tradition, people mainly study three texts on Madhyamaka. One is the *Madhyamakalamkara* by Shantarakshita. Another is *Madhyamakavatara* or *Entering the Way of the Madhyamaka* by Chandrakirti. The third text that people study on Madhyamaka is Shantideva's *Way of the Bodhisattva,* or *Bodhicharyavatara,* especially the ninth chapter.

There are also a lot of less scholarly, yogi-style writings on emptiness. Generally, all the teachings or writings, at least in the Tibetan Buddhist tradition, fall into either the *pandita* style or *kusali* style. A *pandita* is an erudite scholar, and a *kusali* is more like a wandering yogi. You can say that in many ways, Nagarjuna's works on Madhyamaka, as well as Chandrakirti's and Aryadeva's, are in the pandita, or scholarly style.

The teachings and writings that are considered the kusali style are usually experiential, nonconceptual, and easier to understand. Some people appreciate them, while other people don't like them because they are not conceptual enough.

The *Prajnaparamita Sutras* can't be put into any category because they are sutras. We cannot say they are either pandita or kusali style. They are beyond all the categories. We cannot classify them.

Hierarchy of Madhyamaka

There is a type of hierarchy within the Madhyamaka schools. The Tibetans assert that there are two Madhyamaka schools, *Madhyamaka Svatantrika* and *Madhyamaka Prasangika*. The latter one is considered the highest and most supreme, and is the Madhyamaka mainly taught by masters such as Chandrakirti and Shantideva. Tibetans believe that these masters were able to describe the true Madhyamaka exactly the way Nagarjuna taught it.

There are various distinctions between these two schools of thought, and scholars of the past gave their own way of separating them. Yet, if we look into the etymology of their names, we could say the major difference between these two schools of thought is that *Madhyamaka Svatantrika* attempts to give rise to insight in others, such as their opponents, by applying a logical premise that sounds almost intrinsically valid. Whereas *Madhyamaka Prasangika* does not really have its own logical premise that is naturally valid. Rather, it uses the reasoning and logic held by others to show the logical dilemma or erroneous philosophical consequences of that logic, so that others will let go of their wrong philosophy and gain true insight.

The emergence of these two schools of thought started sometime in the fifth century CE when Bhavaviveka attacked Buddhapalita's commentary on Nagarjuna's most important text on Madhyamaka, the *Mula-Madhyamaka-*

Karika. Chandrakirti disagreed with Bhavaviveka, leading to a split between followers of Bhavaviveka (Svantrikas) and Chandrakirti (Prasangikas).

Most Tibetan Buddhist masters, including Lama Tsongkhapa and nineteenth-century Nyingma master Lama Jamgön Mipham, tend to claim that they are the followers of Madhyamaka Prasangika. In fact, Lama Mipham declared that Chandrakirti of India and Rongzom Pandita of Tibet speak with the same mind and same voice since they are both followers of Madhyamaka Prasangika. Chandrakirti is considered one of the main founders of Madhyamaka Prasangika, and Rongzom Pandita is one of the greatest Nyingma masters, along with Longchen Rabjam.

Yet you can say that the Tibetan masters do not really always agree with each other on the philosophy of Madhyamaka Prasangika. This is because there are unresolved differences on many topics, including how to interpret what is called *trö drel (spros bral)*.

Let me translate *trö drel*. It is a very important term, especially in the Nyingma tradition, whether you are studying Madhyamaka, Vajrayana, or Dzogchen. *Trö drel* means freedom from mental proliferation: *trö* means mental proliferation; *drel* means devoid of, or to be free. *Trö drel* and emptiness are almost like synonyms. *Trö drel* is often interpreted as a kind of nonconceptual truth that you can't say anything about. It is beyond all forms of philosophical assertions.

For example, the twentieth-century scholar Gendun Chöpel quoted the famous anecdote of the Flower Sermon where Buddha sat before the gathering not saying anything, as a way of showing that ultimately, you can't say anything about emptiness. Anything you say is just a mental or philosophical assertion. This way of understanding emptiness is found in many Mahayana schools, both in the Tibetan and Zen traditions. However, not all Madhyamaka Prasangika masters hold the view that emptiness is non-conceptual, beyond words.

Treasury of Inquiries

Many of the Madhyamaka teachings are a treasury of inquiries that we can engage with to help us let go of our illusions and attachment to concepts and ideas—not just a few concepts but almost every concept or idea that exists in our head.

Madhyamaka inquiries are also used to show the falsehood of the doctrines developed by various schools of thought in India. For example, when you read a text by Nagarjuna or Chandrakirti, you'll see that they are refuting both non-Buddhist and Buddhist schools of thought. Basically, Madhyamaka teachings show the illusory nature of everything—our concepts and ideas, as well as the doctrines and theories established by the great traditions—so we can let go of attachment to everything, to our own concepts as well as to the doctrines established by the great and sacred lineages.

Some of the inquiries are very complex. They can be quite theoretical and difficult to practice, and you have to get into all their nitty-gritty logic. They are not very enchanting or captivating, they can be convoluted, and some of the logic may not even make sense. So the purpose here is not that we study all the logic and inquiries to gain mastery over them. And yet we would like to get to the heart of all the inquiries.

Basically, Madhyamaka logic is a way of deconstructing our illusions and seeing the silliness and falsehood of our own belief systems, so we can let go of our attachment to them. I am not going to share the convoluted inquiries developed by the Madhyamikas. In a while, we will engage with some of the more simple, practical inquiries and perhaps immediately see an impact on our consciousness. We may see something inside us loosening up. We may feel that we are loosening our grip on our concepts and ideas. We may even feel that immediately on an energetic level.

Emptiness, the Ineffable

In the end, we don't have to reject anything. I think it's really a brilliant idea that negation is a part of all the traditional practices. Even the theistic traditions contemplate what God is not. God is ineffable, so the way to realize the ineffable God is by deconstructing all our concepts that we have about God. But it is not about denying God. It's just that we can understand the true God by dropping all our limiting concepts and ideas about God, in order to experience the ineffable.

I'm not postulating that the ineffable in the theistic tradition and emptiness are the same. Yet it seems that all these traditions have their own way of expressing the ineffable. In Mahayana Buddhism, since there is no God, what is the ineffable? They say the ineffable is emptiness. In the end, the Mahayana tradition says you can't express emptiness, you can't really describe emptiness. This was beautifully described in the hymns by Arhat Rahula to the Great Mother, emptiness. In one verse, he says,

> *You are beyond words, thoughts, beyond all utterance.*
> *You are unborn, you are deathless, like the nature of sky.*
> *You can only be realized by discerning wisdom.*
> *I pay homage to the Mother of the Buddhas.*

You can see clearly in this verse that Rahula says mahashunyata, the great emptiness is, in the end, the ineffable. We can never fully express it in our limited concepts, in our words, in our symbols. At the same time, there is also a path or practice that we can engage in that eventually leads us to the true realization of emptiness as the highest truth.

In the end, it is important to bear in mind that emptiness is not about negating or affirming but is the truth of nonduality. Maybe it can only be experienced in deep silence.

Let's continue with the next paragraph in the *Heart Sutra*.

7

Then noble Avalokiteshvara...

Then noble Avalokiteshvara, the Bodhisattva Mahasattva, said to venerable Shariputra: "O Shariputra, a son or daughter of noble family who wishes to follow the profound path of transcendent wisdom should see in this way: See the five skandhas to be empty of nature."

In the *Heart Sutra*, Avalokiteshvara is the main bodhisattva as well as the one who answers all the questions, even though Buddha himself was presiding. Avalokiteshvara is such an important figure in the *Heart Sutra* that even in the short Chinese version, he is present while Buddha is not even mentioned. Who is Avalokiteshvara?

Can you say Avalokiteshvara is real or unreal? I find both words are limited ways of understanding the ineffable. Can you say, for example, the Great Mother is real or not? Can you say—let's mention the names of some deities—Samantabhadra is real or not? Or can you say Vajrayogini is real or not? Can you say Krodhi Kali is real or not? Krodhi Kali is a dark blue goddess of destruction. But can you say whether she is real or not? We cannot say she is real and we cannot say she is not real either.

If we say she is real, that means we are thinking she is some kind of supernatural being who lies outside of ourselves. That is not actually a true understanding of who she is, and is considered a big error in Tantric Buddhism.

For example, the highest tantra in the Vajrayana tradition, the *Anuttarayoga Tantra*, has two stages: a creation stage (Skt. *utpatti-krama*) and a completion stage (Skt. *sampanna-krama*). The first stage emphasizes creating the mandala of deities and visualizing their forms. However, if we become attached to the form of the deity and anthropomorphize it or turn it into a real entity, this misidentification can bind us rather than liberate us. This error is called *ru drar göl wa* (*ru drar gol ba*), which means falling into the pitfall of Mara.

But we can't say she is not real either. Because when we say she is not real, we are rejecting her. We can't reject Krodhi Kali because Krodhi Kali is an expression of emptiness, or pure awareness. We have to let go of these two ideas—that Krodhi Kali is real or unreal. She goes beyond being either real or unreal. Can you feel that when you say she is real, there is a strong belief in your body that she is outside? But when you say she is not real, you are rejecting something sacred within yourself. Can you feel that energetically? Asserting she is real or not real is a limiting concept.

So Avalokiteshvara goes beyond all kinds of philosophical assertions and all the limits that our mind constructs, such as real or unreal. However, Avalokiteshvara appears as a bodhisattva in the Mahayana sutras. The etymology of his name is "the one who gazes upon all living beings in the world," *Chenrezig* (*spyan ras gzigs*) in Tibetan, *Avalokiteshvara* in Sanskrit. Sometimes Avalokiteshvara is called Lord of the World. *Ishvara* means lord. Avalokiteshvara is the lord of love, the lord of compassion, who loves all living beings in samsara.

In this verse, Avalokiteshvara is referred to as a "Bodhisattva Mahasattva." He is a bodhisattva, but he is also a great bodhisattva, one who has great love, great courage, and great wisdom. This is the definition of Bodhisattva Mahasattva.

One viewpoint says that although both Shariputra and Avalokiteshvara had realized emptiness, they engaged in a conversation for the sake of others. They are teaching in the form of a dialogue, but they are both awakened.

Archetypes for Mind and Wisdom

Even though Shariputra is a historical figure, we can also consider another dimension of Shariputra—that of an archetype. Shariputra is a symbol for our mind, which is inquisitive and has the burning desire to wake up to the wisdom of emptiness.

Similarly, we can think of Avalokiteshvara as an archetype for our inborn wisdom, the transcendent wisdom. There is inborn wisdom in all of us. For example, you may have a question concerning some doubt or confusion regarding life's condition, or about something philosophical. When you sit down and contemplate, eventually wisdom appears in the form of an answer that brings clarity. Through our own reflection, we can see that there is inborn wisdom.

So we can find both Shariputra and Avalokiteshvara as archetypes in our own consciousness. This way of interpreting them is not novel and corresponds with some traditional interpretations.

For example, Shri Singha, the great Indian pandita, composed a commentary on the *Heart Sutra* from the point of view of Tantra, describing the outer, inner, and secret dimensions of the characters and place. He said Rajagriha has the inner meaning of Akanishtha, the highest Buddha paradise, and the secret dimension as one's own awakened awareness. In the same way, he talked about the assembly:

the outer level is the actual monastics and bodhisattvas, and the inner level is *sambhogakaya*, such as the five Buddha families. The secret meaning is nondual, self-aware primordial wisdom.

So it is important not to fixate only on the outer dimension of Shariputra.

Emptiness of All Phenomena

Shariputra asks the question, "How should the bodhisattvas practice the profound path of transcendent wisdom, Prajnaparamita?" Avalokiteshvara starts answering by saying that the way to practice Prajnaparamita is to "see the five skandhas to be empty of nature."

This line is saying that none of the phenomena in the universe have intrinsic nature, whether they are physical or intangible phenomena. We can generally put all phenomena into the categories of tangible or intangible; or we can say form or formless. All the possible phenomena we can comprehend with our consciousness are lacking in intrinsic nature.

Here, the five skandhas are form, feeling, perception, mental formation, and consciousness—which encompass almost everything. As time goes by, we'll look more deeply into how we can understand the notion that all phenomena are empty of intrinsic nature. But before we get into the emptiness of all things, it would be wise to delve into an important topic to pay attention to: no-self.

No Self, No Problem

The line "See the five skandhas to be empty of nature" is actually about no-self, *anatta* in Pali. For many people, no-self is a powerful religious experience. There are mystics in every tradition, not just Buddhism, who reported an experience of no-self. But it seems Buddhism developed an entire philosophical system and set of practices based on the wisdom of no-self.

The whole point of awakening to no-self is to let go of what is called in Tibetan *dak dzin* (*bdag 'dzin*), self-grasping. Buddhism teaches that all our problems and all our misery come from self-grasping. In addition, all the violence in this world, the greed that we see, and the unkindness are somewhat a reflection of this self-grasping.

It seems that in every tradition there are teachings on letting go of self and selfishness. Buddhism teaches that this personal self is not even real in the first place. It is just a fictitious entity. It doesn't exist anywhere.

No-self is a very heated topic among the Buddhists, who do not all have the same way of understanding it. It seems that all the arguments that have gone back and forth on the topics of emptiness and no-self are mostly semantical.

The debates are also about refuting other doctrines of self. For example, Buddhists refute both *atma,* or the doctrinaire self, and the in-born self. The doctrinaire self is more philosophical, while the in-born self is a deeply rooted experience in all of us.

The doctrinaire self, *kün tak kyi dak (kun btags kyi bdag)* in Tibetan, or *atma* in Sanskrit, is understood to have three characteristics: permanent, singular, and independent. It is called the *doctrinaire* self because we are not born with that perception. We have to buy into a certain doctrine, a philosophical belief, to hold the concept of atma, the supreme self, which has those three characteristics. Buddhists negate that version of self. In fact, Buddhists negate not just the self, but any kind of reality that is created by doctrines. The Tibetan term *kün tak* refers to reality that is created merely by doctrine, something that is not there in reality. In that sense, you could say Buddhism negates even the existence of God as the creator, and there are lines of logic in the early Buddhist texts for this negation.

Buddhists also negate what they call *lhen kyé kyi dak (lhan skyes kyi bdag),* which means the in-born or egoic self that comes naturally to everyone at an early age. It is the sense of having a personal self as a primal feeling, without a need to conceptualize it. Every human being somehow develops this egoic perception, believing that we are intrinsically separate from everybody else and that there is a solid personal self, a "me" who is the center of the entire universe. This is just a perception, but it is a perception that happens to everybody.

For example, when you say "I," you are thinking of some kind of continuation of yourself. You were somewhere yesterday—you were at a restaurant, for example—and now you are here. Tomorrow you are going to another place to do something different. It seems there is some kind of personal self that is continuous. Some Tibetan teachers point out that this feeling is what is called the innate self, or inborn self, or inborn ego. But, they say, there is no such thing that continues without changing.

Not only that, there is no self that is separate from our skandhas. Basically, the innate self is the feeling that there is someone in our body who is in control of our body. It feels as if there is a "me" who is separate from our body but who uses the body, who is in charge, who does this and that. It's a feeling that there is a self that is not dependent on the five skandhas. We feel that there are five skandhas and I am the one who is carrying the burden of the skandhas.

Most Buddhists agree that there is no self or person that is independent of the five skandhas. My individuality only exists in relationship to my five skandhas. The characteristic of "person" is a "being-ness" or individuality that comes into being with the five skandhas. The innate ego is the sense that there is a person, "me," who is independent of the skandhas. But if I inquire, there is no person; the "me" only exists in relationship to its five skandhas.

A Ubiquitous Inquiry

The method used in the negation of self is inquiry, which in this case means to look for the self. You'll find this inquiry in almost all the Buddhist teachings—Theravada, Mahayana, Mahamudra, and Dzogchen. It is a ubiquitous inquiry.

In this inquiry, you turn your attention inward to your own body and mind, and try to find your "self" as a concrete, solid entity. You go through a detailed inquiry, trying to find your self in your head, your eyeballs, your throat, your lungs, your kidneys, and so on. Then you try to find your self as the entirety of your body and mind. Buddhism teaches that if you keep inquiring and inquiring in order to find your self, in the end you will not find your self. Then you can have a direct experience of no-self.

There are two versions of emptiness: no-self of person, and no-self of phenomena, which refers to emptiness of everything that exists, including nirvana and the path, down to little things, such as shoes and chairs. One can discover the emptiness of phenomena through the same logic used for emptiness of self. So sometimes different objects are used for inquiry—not just your self but any kind of object.

In the traditional texts, they often used a pillar and vase as examples. Maybe in the olden days, they always needed a vase to get water or as a ritual instrument, and all the houses and temples had pillars. Here we don't really have pillars and vases, but we have this table. We can use this table in front of me as the object of an inquiry.

Usually we tend to believe or automatically perceive that there is a table here. We never question whether this table is real or not. Of course this table is real; there's no doubt. But to what extent is it real? Maybe it is not as real as it appears. When we really look for the table, it turns out that we cannot find any tableness. We cannot find one thing we can say is actually the table. But somehow we end up designating this heap of the different components as "table" and then we agree with each other about our consensus reality. We all agree this is a table.

At the same time, this is not a table until we name it as a table. If we keep inquiring, eventually we cannot find the table or tableness anywhere. Emptiness means things do not exist as specific objects until we label them. This object in front of us does not exist as a table intrinsically, but we think it is a table because we label it as a table. If we keep looking into this table, we'll never find some kind of singular entity or one thing that holds the identity of the table, its "tableness."

Then the logic can get into more detail. One of the meditations you can do in relationship to a table is that you literally say, "What is a table? There's not one thing I can say is a table, but the *whole thing* is a table." Then you meditate and inquire further: "If I remove a nail from a table, is that still a table? Yes, that's still a table. Then my concept of seeing the whole pile of components as a table was wrong." You come to the realization that the whole thing is also not a table if you can remove one part and it is still a table.

This logic can become very detailed, but it does make sense in a weird way. There is not really tableness in any singular part nor in the whole thing. So we can use this detailed inquiry to realize that "table" is just a concept in the end.

There are many ways of understanding how we can use inquiry to realize the emptiness of everything. If I am just talking about emptiness, it may not make too much sense. However, if you have time to sit down and really engage with inquiry, it may make more sense.

In some way, you can say our spiritual path begins when we start inquiring into the nature of everything. Until then, some people would say there is not really a spiritual path. Or at least we can say that the path of awakening starts the moment we don't go along with our consensus reality, which is the *kün dzop kyi den pa* (*kun rdzob kyi bden pa*), the relative truth. We begin to inquire and deeply question the true nature of everything. Have you ever questioned your perceptions? Your thoughts and beliefs about yourself? Your beliefs about reality, about life?

As I said earlier, to me, the whole teaching on emptiness is not just trying to see that things are empty of their true identity. It is a powerful process of letting go. This is how I feel.

Inquiry into Concepts

Another practice we can do is to start questioning all our concepts and beliefs, and see whether they are valid or not. There is an expression in Madhyamaka that says, "Nothing can stand in the face of inquiry." The idea is that if we inquire, the whole reality just collapses. Everything collapses. For example, if you inquire into this table, ultimately the concept of table collapses. Through inquiry, you realize that none of the components are the table nor is the whole heap the table. You realize this thing is a table just because we call it a table. This is an example of why they say everything collapses in the face of inquiry.

Madhyamaka invites all of us to keep inquiring into everything, including buddha mind. Buddha mind is the most sacred concept in Mahayana Buddhism. Yet the Madhyamikas are not saying, "You can inquire into the table or five aggregates because they are not so sacred, but you cannot inquire into notions like *dharmakaya* or buddha mind." They encourage us to inquire into everything, to see that ultimately even dharmakaya is an illusion, buddha mind is an illusion.

This is a very radical understanding. One sutra says, "Even if there is something more exalted than the sublime Dharma, the nirvana, one must regard even that as an illusion and a dream."

In general, we are supposed to inquire into everything—the tathagatagarbha, buddha mind, samyaksambuddha, dharmakaya—no matter how sacred they are. We are supposed to inquire into these things to see whether they are real or not.

Finally, we are supposed to wake up and realize that all the notions we are holding onto—even buddha mind, dharmakaya, tathagatagarbha—are illusory. Madhyamaka says once you inquire, you cannot find anything. Nothing really holds. Everything starts collapsing, like an illusion. Keep in mind that there is nothing too sacred to be inquired into. Are you ready for that?

Emptiness of Self, Emptiness of Other

The view that even tathagatagarbha, buddha nature, is empty brought about a huge debate between what is called *zhen tong* and *rang tong* (*gzhan stong* and *rang stong*). These are two Madhyamaka views known as "emptiness of other" and "emptiness of self." Even these words can sound quite convoluted.

There is a school of thought in Tibetan Buddhism known as Jonang, which continues to exist today in many parts of Tibet. They as well as many masters from other schools hold the zhen tong doctrine. Zhen tong teaches that everything is an illusion, everything is empty, except the tathagatagarbha. They say the ultimate truth, buddha nature, is not empty of itself. Buddha nature is empty of kleshas, empty of delusion, empty of suffering, but it is not empty of itself. It is true, or eternal.

Because this is such a unique position, it has been praised as well as criticized by some scholars from its beginning until now. Some scholars accused this doctrine of having a taint of eternalism. In my understanding, zhen tong and rang tong don't have to be mutually exclusive; zhen tong is also the pure authentic wisdom of Buddha and true Madhyamaka. Both schools of thought look at the same truth but rang tong is using negation, whereas zhen tong is using affirmation. Without the zhen tong view, the truth could get very dry and move into nihilism. I personally feel I am a follower of both.

The earliest critics of the zhen tong doctrine were the famous Tibetan master Butön Rinchen Drup and his followers. Later, the Gelugpa scholars continued the criticism, and it became a fulcrum of the Gelugpa doctrine to criticize that point of view. In the Kagyu tradition many masters such as Jamgön Kongtrul fully embraced the zhen tong doctrine.

When it comes to the Nyingmapas, Lama Mipham can be regarded as the spokesman, and he seems to be a follower of both. He showed that there was a logical way to validate or defend both doctrines.

Not Finding

Lama Tsongkhapa, who wrote many texts on the Prajnaparamita, emptiness, and Madhyamaka teachings, came up with an important and subtle distinction. He said that in inquiry, what you find is not nonexistence of the vase, although you can't find the vase. He said there is a big difference between finding nonexistence of the vase and not finding the vase. He said you'll never find nonexistence of the vase if you inquire into the vase. The vase exists, so you cannot find nonexistence of the vase; that is a denial of reality, that is nihilism. But if you keep inquiring, you will not find the vase. That is emptiness.

Lama Tsongkhapa pointed out two logical faults in general philosophical negation. He called these "too little negation" and "too much negation." Lama Tsongkhapa often accused the Tibetan masters who came before him of falling into the problem of too much negation. He thought the early Tibetan Buddhist masters' way of interpreting emptiness was teetering on nihilism; he accused them of being a little nihilistic and denying reality. He said that in true inquiry, you'll never find nonexistence of everything because nonexistence of something is a total rejection of reality. But he said if you keep inquiring, you'll not find anything. If you keep inquiring into your self, you'll not find your self. But you do exist, he said. You do exist. You are real, but in inquiry you don't find your self. This is a very subtle demarcation that he made.

The idea of not finding something when you look for it is held not only by Lama Tsongkhapa but by many masters in different contexts, such as Madhyamaka, and Dzogchen. For example, Shabkar composed an extraordinary text known as the *Flight of Garuda*, which is a perfect syntheses of Madhyamaka, Mahamudra, and Dzogchen. In that text, he laid out a traditional inquiry into the mind, and then he said, "Not finding is the supreme finding." He said if you look for your mind, in the end you cannot find one thing you can point your finger at and say, "This is my mind." His language is quite witty because we often strive to achieve wisdom and understanding, which is also associated with finding something, such as the truth or wisdom.

To Study or Not to Study

Maybe for some of you, this is too philosophical. But sometimes we should quote these great masters. Otherwise there's nothing to study in terms of the *Heart Sutra* and Prajnaparamita teachings. We can spend the whole day just drumming, chanting, and meditating again and again.

Then noble Avalokiteshvara...

The truth is that some traditions encourage you not to study the scriptures too much. That is even true in some Nyingma traditions. When you go to some meditation retreats in the Nyingma tradition, you are encouraged not to study or even read any books on the topic of your meditation. In some Dzogchen retreats, you may be encouraged to just meditate and practice, and not read any books on Dzogchen.

I heard that there is also a style in the Zen tradition where the teachers encourage you not to study, because they realize that study is limited; you can get a lot of concepts instead of authentic experience. They don't offer an elaborate conceptual commentary on the sutras. Instead, they have you practice a great deal of sitting meditation and periodically chant the sutras. It seems there is more emphasis on how to chant the melody and how to drum than on studying the texts. I appreciate their methods, which have good reasons.

Many years ago, somebody gave me a *Heart Sutra* commentary written by Hakuin, an eighteenth-century Zen master from Japan. I was very excited. I thought it would have a clear conceptual commentary on the *Heart Sutra*, knowing that the *Heart Sutra* is a main liturgy in that tradition. But when I opened it, I was disappointed. In his commentary, Hakuin didn't say anything about the meaning of "form is emptiness," for example. Instead, he said a lot of wild things, such as calling Shariputra funny names. Maybe he realized that you can't say too much about the Prajnaparamita teachings. At that time, I was totally disappointed, but today I can appreciate such a commentary more than ever.

Perhaps this is what the Chinese master Xu Yun was pointing to when he wrote:

> *You've traveled up ten thousand steps*
> *in search of the Dharma.*
> *So many long days in the archives, copying, copying.*
> *The gravity of the Tang and the profundity of the Sung*
> *make heavy baggage.*
> *Here! I've picked you a bunch of wildflowers.*
> *Their meaning is the same*
> *but they're much easier to carry.*

8

Form is emptiness...

Form is emptiness. Emptiness is form. Emptiness is no other than form; form is no other than emptiness. In the same way, feeling, perception, formation, and consciousness are emptiness.

Here, we are working on the emptiness of the first *skandha*, which is form. Some scholars say that the reason the sutras state "form is emptiness" first is because it is easier to realize the emptiness of the other skandhas if we can first realize emptiness of form. There is a perception that form is the thing we are really attached to, the thing we are most identified with. If we realize the emptiness of form, then we can transcend our grasping, our tendency to concretize or reify the other phenomena, such as feeling, perception, formation, and consciousness.

Emptiness of Form

The idea of emptiness of form is very important for our own spiritual path as well as for our inner awakening. We can see that we are bound by our identification with form, which might be material objects, or especially our own body. It would be quite liberating if we could have even a glimpse of the emptiness of our own body, since we are very attached to our own concepts about it.

We can use a Madhyamaka inquiry, or mindfulness of body, *rupa smrti*, as a way to experience emptiness of our body. There are different levels of mindfulness of the body. There is mindfulness of body that is taught in the Theravada tradition and explained to a certain extent in the Tibetan version of the Abhidharma scriptures. Then there is the Mahayana mindfulness of body that focuses on the emptiness of the body. There is also a Tantric mindfulness of body, which is focused on awakening to the sacredness of the body.

Shantideva describes the four foundations of mindfulness from the Mahayana Buddhist point of view in the ninth chapter, the wisdom chapter of his text, *Bodhicharyavatara*. He goes through a whole line of reasoning and logic to show that everything is not as real as it appears. We can read this chapter to better understand how Mahayana uses mindfulness of the body to understand emptiness.

Shantideva has very interesting reasoning to prove that the notion of "body" is an illusion. He invites us to look for our body. Is our head the body? Is our eye the body? Are the inner organs the body? Or is the whole thing the body? And if we end up believing one part is the whole body, he shows the contradiction in such a position.

Emptiness of Feeling

Shantideva also goes into feeling or sensation by asking, "What is feeling?" Feeling doesn't exist, he said. When there is a feeling that we think is real, then we need to question it. When you touch something, you feel an object. For example, when I'm touching this paper, the paper is called *yul (yul)*, object. Shantideva says that for you to really feel that you are touching any object—for example, this paper—your faculty, your skin, has to be in contact with it. *Reg pa (reg pa)* means contact; your faculty has to be in contact with this object.

However, in verse 94 of Chapter 9, Shantideva points out the logic showing this is not possible:

> *If there is space between the sense and its object,*
> *how is there contact between them?*

If there is no space, they are a unity;
Then how is there contact?

So feeling or sensation isn't real because contact isn't possible. This is another kind of logic to prove that things are not as real as we think.

Since the *Heart Sutra* is not one dimensional and can also be interpreted from the Tantric or Vajrayana view, we might like to bring in the notion that feeling, or sensation, is sacred; emptiness of feeling also includes sacredness. For example, Tantric texts have their own version of the four foundations of mindfulness where they say the true nature of your feeling is empty and also sacred.

Inseparable Form and Emptiness

All the Madhyamaka philosophical schools try to define what it means to say "form is emptiness." Our understanding of this line, "form is emptiness," has to do with the idea that form is empty of true identity even though we label something as form.

Then the sutra says, "Emptiness is form." The reason we utter this line, "Emptiness is form," is to counter the very subtle misunderstanding that there may be a separation, a duality, between emptiness and form, such as "form is form" and "emptiness is the true nature of the form." This implies a subtle duality separating form and its true nature.

It is very easy for us to think there is a form and then there is some kind of emptiness hiding somewhere in the form as its true nature. To counter that misunderstanding, the *Prajnaparamita Sutras* always have the two lines "Form is emptiness. Emptiness is form." There is no duality between the form and its true nature.

Then the sutra says, "Form is none other than emptiness, emptiness is none other than form." Avalokiteshvara further emphasizes the inseparability of form and emptiness with these lines. It means that we cannot find emptiness separate from form or form separate from emptiness. So these lines are almost the same.

Even though the four lines seem to be repetitious, they are important philosophically, although perhaps a little convoluted. They are also called the *four integrations of emptiness, tong nyi zhi jor (stong nyid bzhi sbyor)*. These four lines are so dense that in the past, scholars and masters gave extensive teachings on them. Sometimes they used this category of the four integrations as a framework to explain the entire philosophy of emptiness.

These four lines can help us have a fuller understanding of emptiness as well as cut through misconceptions or misunderstandings that may arise. For example, some might accuse the Mahayana Buddhists of turning emptiness into an entity, something like a quasi-deity. Such accusations cannot be applied to the Mahayana tradition, but it is possible that some Mahayana Buddhists may fall into that trap. Unconsciously, they may think emptiness is some kind of Mahayana Buddhist version of a formless divinity, something intrinsically sacred, and separate from everything else.

Some Mahayana Buddhists can also fall into the trap of duality, thinking that emptiness is pure or divine, and everything else, such as the relative truth, is impure. The four integrations of emptiness can help us cut through these misconceptions. These kinds of possible misconceptions must have been an issue from the very beginning because the Mahayana sutras make a point of stating that the relative truth and ultimate truth are the same in their nature. They say this to ensure that we don't develop this kind of subtle dualism.

As we look at these dense lines of the text, we can see that there is some kind of progression in our understanding of ultimate truth, which is expressed in these four lines. The lines show that in the beginning we may inquire into the true nature of form and realize that the form is not intrinsically form. This insight is an understanding of the notion that form is emptiness. But then there is a subtle danger that one can get stuck with the emptiness of form, thinking form is not real, and emptiness is something separate. So these four lines can basically help us to have the complete understanding of the great emptiness, which is the integration of all things that exist and their true nature. Nagarjuna said,

Form is emptiness...

When the relative truth and the ultimate truth are seen
as aspects of each other,
they blend together perfectly
and thus are said to be utterly integrated.

Many Tibetan scholars quote this particular verse to explain the four integrations of emptiness. This verse is quite clear. Nagarjuna is pointing out that the two truths, form and emptiness, are completely inseparable. There is not even the slightest place where they can be separated. Even though form is supposed to be relative truth, and emptiness is the ultimate truth, there is not even the slightest separation between them. The reason there is the duality between the two truths in the beginning is because the relative truth is based on the way we perceive things with our ordinary mind, and the ultimate truth is the way we perceive things through the more awakened mind.

Ultimately, all the explanations have to come to an end because the ultimate truth cannot be fully captured through words and concepts. You need to drop the rational mind in order to experience emptiness. Our human mind has a tendency, a deep-seated habit, to want to grasp at something, even emptiness. It is challenging for us to let go of attachment to anything. And as long as we are attached to something, we may not be able to experience the fullness of emptiness.

The Fragrance of Emptiness

Emptiness is great peace, and form is life, and form and emptiness are inseparable. They are complementary to each other. They are expressions of each other. Without suffering, delusion, and duality, life would not take place in the first place. You and I would not be here right now in this very moment. You and I are here with our life, which is so rich and colorful in itself, with countless moments of sadness, joy, love, and compassion, as well as delusion. This is the fullness of emptiness, expressed in the form of life.

Let's go back to the last line of this paragraph.

9

In the same way...

In the same way, feeling, perceptions, formation, and consciousness are emptiness.

We can now say, "Feeling is emptiness, emptiness is feeling, feeling is none other than emptiness, emptiness is none other than feeling." Even though we don't recite the line in that way, we have to keep in mind that the statement applies to the entire list of dharmas, all phenomena.

Emptiness is a big topic; we are never going to come across a solid or final definition of it. Ultimately it is said that emptiness is not something we can comprehend or conceptualize. At the same time, there are teachings on emptiness, as well as practices such as analytical meditation, and all the reasonings on the definition of emptiness.

All the Buddhist teachers wrote and taught about emptiness from their own understanding. Because of that, there seems to be a philosophical dissonance on the definition of emptiness. That philosophical dissonance happened among both Indian as well as Tibetan Mahayana Buddhists.

Regarding the view of the great emptiness, the big difference between the Gelugpa masters, such as Lama Tsongkhapa, and other great masters, such as Lama Mipham, is that Lama Tsongkhapa and his followers tend to assert that emptiness is something we can express through words and concepts. Whereas Jamgön Mipham and many other Tibetan yogis and panditas say that the true emptiness goes beyond words and concepts.

Many sutras also explicitly state that the ultimate truth of emptiness goes beyond words and concepts. For example, some Mahayana sutras say that the ultimate truth is not knowable to the logicians. To avoid this criticism, Lama Tsongkhapa and his followers interpreted these statements as referring to logicians from other schools, not Mahayana schools.

From the Western point of view, you might regard Lama Tsongkhapa as more of a logician, while Jamgön Mipham is more of a mystic. This is not to say that one is right and the other is not, but it is good to keep in mind that they are looking at the subject from very different points of view: logician versus mystic.

In the same way...

Lama Mipham is perhaps one of the most important philosophers in the Nyingma tradition responsible for reviving the Nyingma academic studies. The early Nyingma masters wrote many teachings on Tantrayana and Dzogchen but not that much on the general Buddhist doctrines, such as Madhyamaka, Abhidharma, logic, and so forth. Lama Mipham was a prolific writer as well as an almost self-taught, brilliant scholar. He wrote many commentaries and books on the Indian texts, and his work quickly became the curriculum at Nyingma monasteries.

Today, his work is regarded as the most important for Nyingma studies. One of his writings was a refutation that went back and forth between two prominent Gelugpa scholars at the time, as a way of bringing light to the unique understanding of Nyingma philosophy, especially at a time when Tibet was taken over by the doctrine of the Gelug school.

The Finite and the Infinite

Emptiness is synonymous with the ultimate truth in the Mahayana tradition. As we know, there are two truths in the Mahayana Buddhist tradition: the relative truth and the ultimate truth. The reality that we perceive with our ordinary mind is the relative truth. It is a reality that is not examined, not investigated. Then, once we are no longer satisfied with our ordinary reality, we begin to inquire, investigate, and analyze the very nature of all phenomena—everything that we feel, experience, and perceive. Then whatever we are going to find through such inquiry is called the ultimate truth.

By the way, there's nothing that is going to be found in the end! So maybe not finding anything that you can hold onto through deep analysis or inquiry is the ultimate truth. In that sense, the ultimate truth is not some kind of thing about which we can say, "Oh, this is the nature of reality. Only this is real; everything else is unreal, illusion."

The two truths are needed in order to bring some kind of balance between the finite and infinite. Some modern thinkers criticize the early masters for coming up with the two truths. But they are missing the point of the brilliant minds of the early ones. With these two truths, we can avoid falling into any kind of philosophical trap, such as rejecting transcendence or rejecting the world and this human life. The Prajnaparamita teachings are inviting us to embody the realization of emptiness in a way that doesn't reject the relative truth.

Lama Tsongkhapa, perhaps one of the greatest minds that Tibet produced, said that emptiness is not nothingness. He said you cannot reject the relative truth. You cannot reject the world of existence. What he said was that if you look for anything, you'll not find it. If you look for a table, for example, or the glass of water in front of me, eventually you'll not find it.

In the same way...

Let's review this again. He gave a very clear example. He used a vase as an example. He said to imagine you are analyzing or investigating the true nature of a vase by asking, "What is this vase? Is the vase real or not? Is it an illusion or concrete?" He said that after deep inquiry, you'll not find nothingness or nonexistence of the vase but you'll not find a vase either. This turns out to be a very important statement. It is perhaps one of the best statements on emptiness; it clarifies and cuts through a lot of misconceptions and pitfalls regarding the realization of emptiness.

What he means is that through deep inquiry, if you come across nothingness or nonexistence of the vase, this indicates that there is no vase. In his mind, that is considered nihilism. Obviously there is a vase. There is everything—there is a house, there is a road, there is a street, there are mountains and rivers. There is you and there is me. Emptiness does not mean nothingness. Nothingness means there is nothing there.

In the same way, if you turn the scope of inquiry toward yourself, you can look for your "self," but in the end, you will not find your self. This does not mean that you don't exist. He is saying that if you turn the scope of inquiry toward yourself to find out who you are by simply asking, "Who am I? What is the self? Where is the self located?" you will not find your self in the end. There is no self that you are going to find. But he is also saying you are not going to find nonexistence of yourself because obviously you exist.

In the same way, you can look deeply into your own body. Is your body real or an illusion? According to Lama Tsongkhapa, if you keep inquiring, you are never going to find the nonexistence or nothingness of your body because your body exists. It is a phenomenon, it exists. But you are also never going to find one thing that is your own body, something you could point to and say, "This is my body."

Lama Tsongkhapa's statements are a conservative way of illuminating emptiness so that there is no danger of falling into nihilism. According to Madhyamaka, most people who don't follow the path of inquiry fall into the trap of eternalism. But then, once somebody starts practicing inquiry and starts examining and questioning the nature of all things, there is also a danger of falling into the trap of nihilism, thinking that nothing really exists.

So you see that emptiness is very delicate, indeed. It is not really an obvious topic where we can say right away, "Oh, this is emptiness."

Subtle Refinements

A famous Indian pandita, a bhikshu named Shantarakshita, a contemporary of Guru Padmasambhava, came to Tibet during the eighth century. He wrote a well-known text on Madhyamaka, *Madhyamakalamkara*, which means *Ornament of Madhyamaka*.

There is a verse in this text that seems to be quite important in terms of further separating the subtle and gross levels of our understanding of emptiness or ultimate truth. It says:

> *In actuality, nothing whatsoever exists.*
> *Therefore, the Tathagata said, "All things are unborn."*
> *Because this truth is in harmony with the ultimate truth,*
> *the unborn is also labeled the ultimate truth.*
>
> *In actuality, the ultimate truth is liberated*
> *from the host of mental elaborations.*
> *Because there is no such thing as birth and so forth,*
> *even "unborn" is impossible.*

This verse divides the realm of ultimate truth into two further categories: the *approximate ultimate truth*, in Tibetan, *nam drang pé dön dam* (rnam grangs pa'i don dam), and the *actual ultimate truth*, in Tibetan, *dön dam tsen nyi pa* (don dam mtshan nyid pa). These are further subtle categories for our understanding of the ultimate truth.

The approximate ultimate truth is the truth that can be expressed in words. Shantarakshita is saying that the actual ultimate truth is ineffable and not something we can put into words and concepts. Even the notions of unborn and no-self are concepts because they are based on negation. At least this is how Lama Mipham and other Tibetan masters interpret this verse because they also hold the position that the ultimate is ineffable. We must remember that Lama Tsongkhapa and his followers would interpret this verse in a way that would validate their own position, which is that emptiness is not ineffable.

This is fascinating; you have to be aware that these great Tibetan scholars throw contrasting interpretations on the same text, whether it is a shastra by the Indian panditas or a sutra. This is why a famous proverb that developed in the Tibetan culture says, "Both scriptures and deerskin can be pulled or twisted in any direction you want."

From my point of view, Lama Mipham and some of the other Tibetan masters are in some way much more in literal alignment with the sutras and shastras, whereas Lama Tsongkhapa made a major reinterpretation of the sutras and shastras. This is why Gendun Chöpel later accused Lama Tsongkhapa's followers of having a bit of a double-standard since they revered the Buddha's words and the words of the Indian panditas, but they always criticized their Tibetan peers and scholars. Gendun Chöpel said that if you want to refute the Tibetan scholars, refute them along with the Buddha, because in the literal sense, they say the same thing as the Buddha.

The major disagreement between the early Tibetan scholars and their followers with Lama Tsongkhapa's

In the same way...

followers, is that the latter somehow hold the stance that everything, including ultimate truth, has to be logical, rational, and conceptual, because otherwise it won't make sense. They always want to be sure that things make sense. Anything that doesn't make sense is regarded as hocus-pocus. Whereas the early Tibetan scholars and Lama Mipham hold the stance that the ultimate truth is transcendent, in the sense that it is indescribable. They say this is why our rational mind can't capture the ultimate truth fully, no matter how profound or subtle our mind might be. They support the idea that the ultimate truth is nonconceptual. Jigme Lingpa, in one of his Dzogchen dohas, said,

> *Taking sides on existence or nonexistence completely collapses.*
> *Even Buddha's tongue gets stuck when uttering this truth.*

Here, Jigme Lingpa is basically telling us that emptiness is, in the end, totally ineffable, and not something that can be easily put into words. This expression of Jigme Lingpa reminds us of the *Flower Sermon*, where Buddha didn't say even one word.

Some intellectuals from the Gelug tradition have also written refutations on the Madhyamaka taught by Nyingmapas and Kagyupas. They also refute Dzogchen and Mahamudra for the same reason—that they are too nonconceptual and not built upon solid logic, even though this is not true. At the same time, other individuals in the Gelug tradition are open to the nonconceptual teachings, such as Dzogchen. For example, the fifth Dalai Lama was outwardly a Gelugpa but inwardly he practiced the Nyingma teachings.

This philosophical conflict will not be solved easily and may remain for a long time, even though there is an idea in the Tibetan tradition that all these teachings ultimately speak the same truth. Well-known masters used reasoning to show that all the traditions speak the same truth, in the same way that all rivers eventually merge into the ocean. In my opinion, all the different views presented by various Tibetan schools of thought are valid in themselves, so we cannot say one is right and one is wrong. It seems that we need all their views to really see the complete picture of the ultimate truth.

In the end, the ultimate truth is ineffable. It is not something that we can conceptualize or capture in the realm of the intellectual mind. In the *Prajnaparamita Sutras*, Buddha said again and again that the ultimate truth goes beyond words and concepts. He was quite emphatic about this.

Beyond Mind

A Buddha sat
Before a sermon
Without words.
Pure silence and a smile.

There are no "isms" in that silence.
No words can describe it.
No philosophy can capture it.
The nihilist,
The eternalist,
What do they know anyway?

When mind stops, there is great peace.
It goes beyond knowing and not knowing.
It doesn't belong to anyone,
Love pours out of it.
Compassion flows from it.

The Fragrance of Emptiness

Hold a rose flower,
Its beauty is free.
Gaze upon it and
Put aside your ideologies.
Be enchanted by it.
Be speechless.
It will show you the beauty of life.

This fragile flower,
You must hold it gently.
Don't say it's good or bad,
Let it reveal its magic to you.
Soon it will decay.

Let's meet together in a field where there is no mind,
There we can test a nameless peace.
Some call it great emptiness.

Right now, let your thoughts go,
Take a few deep breaths and
Drink the nectar of beauty around you.

Tomorrow when the sun rises,
Remember to go outside.
Stretch your arms to the sky,
Give a long sigh,
Let the warmth touch your skin and whisper to yourself,
"I am alive."

10

Negation, A Stage on the Path

It seems that there are hierarchical stages of awakening in relationship to emptiness. Or we can say there are different levels of awakening to emptiness. In the beginning, it is said, individuals cannot realize nonduality right away because it is the ultimate truth, the highest truth, or the actual ultimate truth, in the language of Shantarakshita.

Who are the individuals this statement is referring to? We can call them yogis. In the opening of the ninth chapter, the wisdom chapter, of *Bodhicharyavatara*, Shantideva said there are two worlds—the world of ordinary individuals and the world of yogis. Here, *yogi* refers to somebody who meditates, who inquires, who is awakened, or who at least is not completely deceived by the seeming reality that is constructed by his or her own concepts and ideas. Or a yogi is one who is awakened or who is teetering on the brink of awakening. Sometimes in the Buddhist teachings, *yogi* also refers to somebody who has some kind of direct experience of the ultimate truth, no-self, or emptiness, not just someone with a lot of rich knowledge.

The term *yogi* means more than someone who is spiritual or religious; it is someone who meditates and inquires into the true nature of reality. Once we start meditating and deeply inquiring into the nature of all things, with an existential questioning, then our previous illusions begin to crumble. We see a whole new version of reality that is perhaps more liberating.

It's a fascinating idea that Shantideva offers—that there are two worlds within this world. Even though we are all living in one physical world, because we live in different mental states, it is as if we are living in different worlds, with different perceptions of reality. You could have ten people underneath one roof, and they could all see things differently. Someone could be very angry, seeing everything in life as bad, at the same time that someone else could be in bliss, seeing sacredness everywhere.

Even though these perceptions sound impersonal, abstract, they do have a direct impact on your experience, in terms of your personal happiness and your personal suffering. If you believe this world is unfriendly, this world is a danger zone, that would immediately influence your state of mind and bring about paranoia, pain, and contraction. But if you believe this world is lovely, benevolent, and if you believe humanity is intrinsically good, then in everyday life, you will feel more joy, love, and trust.

This idea is illustrated by a parable from one of the sutras. During a sermon, Buddha invited the audience to share their perceptions of the world. An individual named Brahma Sikkim reported, "I see the world as equal to the splendor of the abodes of the highest deities." Then Buddha asked Shariputra what he saw, and Shariputra said, "I see this great earth, with its highs and lows, its thorns, its precipices, its peaks, and its abysses, as if it were entirely filled with excrement." That was his answer. It sounds very depressing, doesn't it? "That's all I see in this world." Basically, there was nothing inspiring about this human world, this earth, to him. All he saw through his distorted perception was a world that was ugly, impure, filled with all these disenchanting and ugly ingredients and substances.

Buddha touched the ground with his big toe, and suddenly Shariputra's vision was transformed. Then the Buddha said to the venerable Shariputra, "Shariputra, now what do you see?" Shariputra replied, "I see splendor such as I never before heard of or beheld!" Buddha said to Shariputra, "The fact that some living beings do not behold the splendid display of virtues in the world is due to their own ignorance. The universe is always pure, but you do not always see it."

This inspiring anecdote tells us that as individuals, we live in our own mental states and worlds, and project them onto reality, thinking that what we perceive is the way things are. The idea is that the more we become awakened spiritually, the more we can see the way things are, and we are less deluded. This automatically brings about more peace and joy.

This parable is also saying that awakened yogis can see the world as sacred. Here, sacred is not some kind of intrinsic reality. Sacred in Tibetan is *dag pa (dag pa)*—pure, purified, similar to the term *devoid of*. Things are devoid of being imperfect, impure, or flawed. Once we realize that things don't have intrinsic flaws, then maybe naturally we experience some kind of religious love toward everything, or reverence. Such an experience is often described as pure vision, the sacred outlook, in Tantric Buddhism.

In my tradition, they say that true, pure perception only arises when you experience emptiness. Otherwise, if you start telling yourself the wonderful narrative that "everything is sacred," sacredness becomes another concept. Then you have a lot of ideas about what being sacred, pure, or divine means. It becomes just another big concept, another golden chain inside you. This golden chain has bound many people throughout history. So this sacred outlook, the pure vision, only arises when you know how to drop all your perceptions, all your concepts, and know how to open your heart and feel the vibrancy, the magic of right now, of this world, this life, this universe, this smell, this sound, this form, this color.

Bhumis – Stages on the Path

The yogi will go through different stages of awakening as a result of his or her initial inner awakening. This reminds us that inner awakening is a process. It is not as if you wake up spiritually, and then there is no more evolution. This is why the Mahayana tradition came up with the ten *bhumis* (*sa* in Tibetan), the ten grounds of awakening. These refer to the inner, gradual spiritual evolution. In general, we can say there are evolutionary stages of consciousness, which are described in three ways in the Mahayana tradition. For example, the *Uttaratantra* says,

> *Impure, pure-impure, and*
> *utterly perfectly pure are successive.*
> *In the same way, beings are called*
> *sentient beings, bodhisattvas, and Tathagatas.*

This is saying that, in general, there are three stages of consciousness. The first is obviously the consciousness of sentient beings, whose consciousness might be lost, not purified, and shrouded in the thickness of kleshas. Then there are the bodhisattvas, who are quite purified but not completely. They are purified in comparison to the deluded ones but not in comparison with the *samyak-sambuddhas*.

They are at a level in between those two types of beings. The last level is the Tathagata, or Buddha, fully awakened and purified of obscurations. This tells us that we all live in different stages of consciousness. We will all have a different sense of the reality we live in, due to our mental state.

As a teaching, Prajnaparamita has two aspects. One aspect is simply the teachings on emptiness. Another aspect is the elaborate teachings on the stages a yogi goes through when he or she starts having the experience of awakening to the great emptiness. It is said that Buddha clearly taught the great emptiness in the *Prajnaparamita Sutras*, but he didn't teach the bhumis, or stages of awakening, in relationship to emptiness as clearly. Achyara Asanga wrote many treatises to illumine the stages of awakening, or the inner evolution, that a yogi goes through in relationship to the great emptiness.

Acharya Asanga's text *Abhisamayalankara*, the *Ornament of Realization*, is considered the main text on the stages of awakening. Tibetans wrote numerous commentaries on this text, and the topic is considered one of the most important topics to study in Tibetan monasteries. The Sakya and Gelug schools have made a heavy investment in the study of *Abhisamayalankara*. Later, the Nyingma school also started taking this topic seriously. A famous Nyingmapa scholar from the twentieth century, Dongak Tenpé Nyima, wrote quite an extensive text on the stages of awakening in accordance with *Abhisamayalankara*. His writing was the beginning of the serious study of *Abhisamayalankara* in the Nyingma tradition, where it is now incorporated as a major topic of study in Nyingma monasteries.

The Tantric tradition has its own version of the bhumis, known as the sixteen bhumis. Each of the bhumis has very specific qualities. We can learn about them by going back to the shastras. At the same time, we cannot get very attached to the literal interpretation of the bhumis.

There's a funny story that tells of a debate about the bhumis. In the Mahayana shastras, it is said that when you reach the first bhumi and see the great emptiness, you are able to travel to one hundred buddha paradises, you can meet with one hundred buddhas, and you can emanate yourself to one hundred worlds as a bodhisattva to help others. It seems that when the great Sakya Pandita was alive (twelfth century), he noticed that the Mahamudra and Dzogchen practitioners were claiming they were awakened. He was disturbed since he thought they should have all those miraculous signs, and he criticized the ubiquitous claims of awakening as questionable or false.

The Mahamudra master Drikung Jigten Sumgön responded to his criticism by saying that if people showed those signs, it meant they reached the first bhumi, but if they didn't show those signs, it was not evidence they hadn't reached the bhumi. If you reach the first bhumi, you don't always have those signs. He said, "If anybody finds one sutra or tantric text that says that if people don't show those signs, it is proof they haven't reached the first bhumi, I will give him a horse adorned with silks," which at that time was a rare and valued gift.

So we can't get attached to the signs of awakening mentioned in the sutras. There may be people in modern days who have profound awakenings but don't display siddhis or miracles. That does not mean their awakening is not authentic.

The marks of awakening are very hard to determine. At the same time, it is also important to have some checks and balances about claims to awakening. Even today, many people claim they had a spiritual awakening, or they are awakened. The question is whether we should trust all of them or discard all these claims. My thought is that we can't do either. If we trust all of them, we could be fooling ourselves as well as allowing others to be fooled. But if we discard them, we are shutting down any kind of profound human epiphany, which could be a denial of our human potential. Maybe there are not particular signs that allow us to say, "This is an indication that someone is awakened." But at the end of the day, if we feel someone is authentically compassionate and selfless, then we can trust that person's claims. We also must use our own intelligence and common sense regarding whether we trust someone's claims.

Negation, A Stage on the Path

The stages of the path are also very inspiring, because they tell us that we can continue to evolve and grow. So it is very positive.

Why Negation?

When you read the *Heart Sutra*, you see that it is full of negation. Why is there so much negation in Buddhism, especially in Mahayana Buddhism?

Many years ago, I met with some monks at the Catholic monastery in Big Sur. They invited me to have a conversation with them, and we had a very nice dialogue. One monk connected with me, and visited me in the Santa Cruz mountains at a Buddhist center. During his visit, we had an interfaith conversation where he shared that when he heard someone reciting the *Heart Sutra*, he didn't like it because there was so much negation. He felt it was a little bit cold-hearted and there was no grace or blessing or divinity in the language because it was all negation.

Perhaps he heard the *Heart Sutra* that we are reciting. It's full of negations—"no eye, no nose, … no attainment, no wisdom." And this is just the *Heart Sutra*, which is really short. Imagine if you were reading the huge volumes of the *Prajnaparamita Sutra*. You'd spend days and days reciting words of negation.

It might be true that some religious traditions don't use the method of negating in relationship to the absolute or divine; clearly this monk was not very comfortable with it.

As we've said earlier, negation is not always enticing for us. Especially as spiritual people, we love language that is based more on affirmation. Love, compassion, grace, blessing, achievement, enlightenment, salvation, nirvana, liberation—when you think of these spiritual topics, they are all affirmations. There is very little negation in them. Love is not negation. Compassion is not negation. Achievement is not negation. Attainment is not negation. The divine is not negation. So we may sometimes feel that negation is lacking in spiritual richness or even divinity.

And yet a very essential part of spirituality is letting go—letting go of our attachment, our ego, our self, our greed, and our hatred. Letting go is almost a golden principle of all spiritual traditions. In a very profound sense, negation is nothing more than a form of letting go. Here negation is an invitation to let go of our attachment to our concepts, our opinions, our belief systems, and our usual version of reality.

As time goes by, we will actually find the great emptiness is profoundly rich. The Jonang tradition as well as the Nyingma and Kagyu traditions emphasize the idea that emptiness is not just negation. It is full of everything—full of divinity, full of the Dharmas, full of love, full of sacredness. We'll talk about those things as

Negation, A Stage on the Path

time goes by. So why do the sutras use negation again and again?

The idea is this: *ngö poi du shé chen* (*dngos poi 'du shes can*). Let me try to translate the Tibetan words into English: *ngö po* means thing or realness, *du shé* means perception, and *chen* means to possess. It means "those with a perception of realness."

This means that as human beings, we have a deep-seated dualistic perception—or dualistic thinking—that grasps at everything as being real. It turns out that many of our struggles come from this. We perceive everything as real and concrete. We perceive ourself as real, our body as real. We perceive happiness and suffering, the whole world of phenomena, to be real. We basically experience everything—good, bad, right, wrong, nirvana, samsara, you, me—as real.

Many Mahayana and Tantric Buddhist practices are designed to cut through our tendency to reify the phenomenal world. One of my favorite verses that expresses this spirit is from a *Chöd* liturgy called *The Dakini's Laughter* by Jigme Lingpa. A verse on developing bodhichitta says:

Through the yogi's conduct,
In order to obliterate
the mind that grasps appearances as real,

and to realize the true way of things,
without hope and fear, I shall give rise to bodhichitta.

This verse captures the heart of the *Prajnaparamita Sutras*, which makes sense since the entire Chöd practice is based on these sutras. We might like to go back to this verse and look at the words *appearances*, *nang wa (snang pa)*, and *grasping to be real, ngö por dzin pa (dngos por dzin pa)*. These two concepts are quite important. Here, *appearances* refers to anything that exists. To quote a verse from Tilopa's advice to Naropa,

My son, appearances do not bind you, but grasping at them does.
Oh Naropa, cut through the grasping.

Tilopa is saying things do not really bind us; the world, life, birth, death don't bind us. But when we grasp at things and concretize or reify them, then we end up being bound by our own mind. So the *Heart Sutra* is a way of letting go of our grasping and attachment.

No Assertions

Madhyamaka, or Prajnaparamita, is not trying to come up with any kind of unchangeable assertion, not saying things do exist or do not exist. In the end, Madhyamaka goes beyond all concepts. Nagarjuna expressed his understanding of emptiness in a famous verse:

I have no assertions.
Because of that, I am flawless.

He is saying that there is no view that he holds onto. This is considered the utmost manifesto on the highest insight. This verse can be considered the foundation of Madhyamaka Prasangika philosophy.

Ultimately, the *Prajnaparamita Sutras* are not trying to convince us that everything is unreal but are just helping us loosen our grasping and our dualistic perception that everything is real. As a famous Madhyamaka saying goes, "It is neither existence nor nonexistence." If you really end up believing that everything is unreal, that can fall into the assertion of nonexistence, which is another trap, a nihilistic trap.

Furthermore, it's quite important at this point in talking about negation to once again see what we are negating. There are different ways of identifying what is to be negated. But when we become abstract and philosophical about what is to be negated, then the negation doesn't have any impact on our ability to let go and become free. Such negation becomes a philosophical game that has little merit. We can negate many things in our head that have no relevance to our present life. Then it is really no more than a mental game.

Yet there is a strong philosophical dissonance among Tibetan masters in terms of identifying what is to be negated. For example, the Gelugpas tend to have some resistance to negating anything that is immediate and right in front of them. So they usually talk about negating notions of true existence or the true identity of things. Yet among Gelugpa masters, some individuals might even challenge the way many Gelugpas understand Madhyamaka. One of them is Changkya Rölpé Dorjé, who was a brilliant scholar and linguist from the eighteenth century. He spoke many languages and served as a tutor to the Manchu emperor. He wrote a *doha*, or a song of realization, on Madhyamaka that Lama Mipham found to be so profound that he wrote a whole commentary on it. A verse in that doha says:

Leaving these vivid appearances alone,
and looking for something else with a horn to be negated,
there is a danger that the Old Mother may run away.

This is a great verse with some humor and quite friendly criticism, regarding the fact that some people don't negate something right in front of themselves and instead reach for some ideal thing to transcend. By the way, the Old Mother is used as a simile for emptiness. Perhaps he called emptiness "Old Mother" because emptiness is depicted as Yum Chen Mo, the great mother.

Let's say you are looking at your smartphone and are about to meditate on the emptiness of the smartphone with deep inquiry. Now, you have to negate something in relationship to the emptiness of the smartphone. What do you negate? If you say, "I'm going to negate the true existence of the smartphone," it won't help remove your grasping to your ideas, concepts, and perceptions of the smartphone. So you have to negate the smartphone. You have to say, "This object in front of me is not a smartphone." You might like to hold it in front of you and shout loudly, "This is not a smartphone." Just don't say that in the store when you are about to purchase one, as they may not get your humor or perception of awakening to the great emptiness. Or remember not to say "This is not food" if somebody invites you to dinner. They might misunderstand you, even though you are saying something truly profound.

One time a spiritual community invited me to teach, and after the meditation retreat was complete, they gave me a gift of a cup with the caption written on it, "This is not a cup." I loved that gift and felt it was the *Heart Sutra* on that cup in an inconspicuous fashion.

11

Negating Through Metaphors and Reasoning

Traditionally, both metaphors as well as reasoning were used to negate not existence but the intrinsic realness or duality of all phenomena. Now and then in the Pali sutras, Buddha brings metaphors or analogies to challenge our usual perception of seeing many things as intrinsically real or true. A famous verse found in the Pali sutras says:

Form is like a lump of foam,
feeling is like a water bubble,
perception is like a mirage,
mental formations are like a hollow tree, and
consciousness is like illusion.

In general, spiritual teachings often use analogies, stories, and parables to make a point. Metaphors and analogies can have a particular kind of power to penetrate our mind in a way that gives rise to profound insight. Sometimes we may have difficulty understanding certain concepts because we are unfamiliar with them. It takes time for our brain to absorb a completely new concept; relating to a metaphor helps our brain figure out the concept more readily. On the other hand, sometimes our brain might have a resistance or strong objection to some concept we don't agree with. When we can relate the concept to a metaphor, we can open our mind and let this new idea enter into our consciousness. This is the power of using metaphors. This is why Buddha always used similes and parables in his sermons.

Metaphors are used in the teachings and practices to show us that things are not as real as the way we experience them. The metaphors are actually a form of negation even though there is no negation in the words. They negate the intrinsic or dualistic reality of all phenomena.

Metaphors for Illusion

As a matter of fact, Buddhism has the famous *twelve metaphors for illusion*, known in Tibetan as *gyu mé wé* (*sgyu ma'i dpe*).

Here is the entire list:

Negating Through Metaphors and Reasoning

1. Illusion
2. Reflection of moon in water
3. Hallucination
4. Mirage
5. Dream
6. Echo
7. City of Gandharvas
8. Magic, like a trick
9. Rainbow
10. Flash of lightning
11. Water bubbles
12. Image in the mirror

These twelve metaphors are used in the Buddhist teachings to indicate that maybe everything is not so real, maybe everything is an illusion.

These days, we have amazing and powerful analogies, especially because of technology, which we can use to describe everything as an illusion or to say that everything is more like a dream. For example, movies are a very good analogy to show that this whole world of phenomena can be unreal, or like virtual reality.

Using analogies and metaphors to point out that everything is an illusion is quite profound and can be understood from different angles and perspectives. However, we must relate cautiously to this notion; we need to know what Buddha really means when he says everything is illusion. Otherwise, if we get lost in our own preconceived notions and our ideas, we can have some serious philosophical misadventures and end up basically being nihilistic. For the time being, we can remember to use these analogies and metaphors to let go of our tendency to reify things, our tendency to get attached to things, rather than get hung up on the idea that everything is an illusion.

Direct negation and metaphors of illusion have the same purpose. In the *Heart Sutra*, we are working with direct negation; for example, we come across words such as "no eye, no nose." Then there are other texts that negate using the twelve metaphors to say that everything is illusion.

Obviously sutras and early shastras used these metaphors of illusion to convey emptiness, or the unreal nature of all things. Later, these metaphors were further elaborated in Vajrayana and Dzogchen. For example, Longchenpa wrote a Dzogchen text known as *Resting in the Illusion of Things*, which has eight chapters. Each chapter corresponds to one of eight metaphors of illusion to show that everything is lacking in *svabhava*.

Some masters used the eight metaphors to negate what are called the *eight extremes of mental proliferations*, or in Tibetan, *trö pé ta gyé (spros pa'i mtha' brgyad)*: arising and ceasing, nonexistence and permanence, coming and going, being multiple and being single. This negation closes down the possibility that things can truly exist in any dimension. They say:

Negating Through Metaphors and Reasoning

*Arising is like a dream; that's why it does not exist.
Ceasing is like an illusion; that's why it does not exist.
Nonexistence is like a reflection of a moon in water;
that's why it does not exist.
Being permanent is like a mirage; that's why it does not exist.
Coming is like a cataract on the eye; that's why it does not exist.
Going is like an echo; that's why it does not exist.
Being multiple is like the city of Gandharvas;
that's why it does not exist.
Being single is like magic; that's why it does not exist.*

Negating Doctrines Through Reasoning

Now let's look at reasoning. In Tibetan, it is called *ten tsik* (*gtan tshigs*) or *rigpa* (*rigs pa*). Buddha himself used some of these reasonings along with metaphors to show that everything is an illusion. Yet Buddha's use of reasoning may not be as extensive as the vast treasury of reasonings found in the shastras or the Madhyamaka commentaries, especially those by Nagarjuna.

As I said earlier, it turns out that these reasonings are extremely subtle, detailed, and can be unbelievably cumbersome for most people. They don't really work with our mindset, unless you become a monk or nun and have nothing else to do in your life. Then you may have all the extra hours, days, and months to work on the texts, learn all the reasonings, and find some merit in them. Some of these reasonings, however, are quite good.

From the highest understanding, when Madhyamikas use reasonings, they are not using them to postulate or to solidify their own view or position because they have no position. As we said earlier, *Madhyamaka Prasangika* has no positions, has no assertions. Instead, they use reasoning to defeat or falsify the positions and views, either eternalism or nihilism, held by all the other schools.

In general, our perception of the nature of things is tainted by our own ignorance and delusion. Even our consensus reality, which we all believe to be true, is found to be based on delusion when we inquire. In addition to that, we create philosophical doctrines that form new kinds of mental illusions. Shantarakshita, a master from the *Madhyamaka Svatantrika* tradition, wrote the famous text, *Madhyamakalamkara*, the *Ornament of Madhyamaka*. At the very beginning of that text, one verse states that the goal of his work is to show the falsehood of almost all the things held as true by both the Buddhists and non-Buddhist schools of thought. The verse says:

> *All these things postulated by ourselves (Buddhists) and others,*
> *in actuality are devoid of being either one or many.*
> *Because of this,*
> *they have no intrinsic existence, and are like reflections.*

Negating Through Metaphors and Reasoning

Here he is saying that the whole Madhyamaka work is to deconstruct the idea of intrinsic nature or intrinsic validity in all things, both in the ordinary world as well as in doctrines.

Periodically, the Madhyamikas target some Vedic philosophical schools as their opponents. But most of the time, their opponents are actually Buddhist schools, especially the other three Buddhist philosophical tenets.

There were four early Indian Buddhist schools, or philosophical tenets—two non-Mahayana schools, known as *Vaibhashika* and *Sautantrika*; and two Mahayana schools: *Chittamatra*, the Mind-Only school, and Madhyamaka. Madhyamaka, especially Madhyamaka Prasangika, takes almost every other Buddhist philosophical school as its opponent because the first three of the four philosophical tenets are considered realists or in Tibetan, ngö por mawa (dngos por smra ba). Ngö por means real, mawa means to assert. Ngö por mawa, or realists, are those who assert that there is intrinsic realness.

The Vaibhashika believe that there is indeed realness. They believe in the realness of the smallest particles. The Sautrantika also believe and teach that there is intrinsic realness; they also say there is a smallest particle that you cannot divide. They debate quite a lot about particles because they wonder about the foundation of this concrete world.

Chittamatrins do not teach that there is a particle; they do not believe there is any external thing. They came up with amazing logic and reasoning to show a contradiction in the idea that there is a smallest particle as the foundation of existence. But then they hold onto the idea that there is a consciousness that is real. So in that sense, they are still considered realists.

Even today, many spiritual people and philosophers in the West tend to embrace the idea that everything is consciousness, somehow thinking that consciousness is the primary phenomenon, while matter or the physical world is the epiphenomenon. From the Madhyamaka Prasangika point of view, this is still dualistic, and can be regarded as a doctrine of the realists. By thinking that consciousness is everything, even though they transcend the material reality, they do not transcend the inherent reality of consciousness.

Letting Go of Concepts and Doctrines

Remember that the method used by Madhyamaka Prasangika to refute other Buddhist schools of thought is not to defend its own position but instead to show contradiction in the other doctrines. The idea is that eventually by seeing contradictions, the others would let go of identification with their doctrine; at least, that's the hope. But the world proves that it is not really easy for

Negating Through Metaphors and Reasoning

people to let go of their identification with their doctrines. People still hold on to their doctrines, possibly because they are attached to them or they find some kind of safety or security in them.

This is illustrated by a very funny story that I heard about the fictional character Nasrudin. Once Nasrudin firmly believed he was a dead man and no one was able to sway him; his friends and relatives all tried but no one had success in changing his mind. When somebody would say, "Nasrudin, let's go out and eat Chinese food," Nasrudin would say, "No, dead men don't go out to eat Chinese food." If someone would say, "Let's go to a movie," Nasrudin would say, "No, dead men don't go to the movies."

Finally somebody brought him to a psychiatrist. The psychiatrist, instead of trying to convince Nasrudin that he was delusional, said to him, "Keep chanting this phrase as a mantra: Dead men don't bleed." Nasrudin liked that request, and he went home and kept reciting "Dead men don't bleed." The next time he went to the psychiatrist, the psychiatrist was hiding behind the door. As Nasrudin walked in repeating, "Dead men don't bleed," the psychiatrist poked Nasrudin's finger with a needle. His finger started to bleed, and Nasrudin said, "Oh, indeed...dead men *do* bleed!"

Even when our doctrines and concepts are proven to be absurd, we tend to stubbornly hold onto them out of habit, or fear of the unknown. Maybe the world periodically needs some radical spiritual masters who tear down our beliefs. Maybe we need that now and then. The job of these teachers may be the hardest job; I don't think many people will like them. Buddha was a radical spiritual master in his time who upset a lot of religious people and priests. Throughout history, in every tradition, there are some radical teachers who have enough wisdom and courage to shake people's dogma. Some of them are often misunderstood, and even murdered and killed.

For example, in the beginning, many of the Mahayana masters and mahasiddhas were misunderstood by some Buddhists. One mahasiddha was Milarepa. Milarepa often expressed the ultimate truth in his teachings. However, since he was teaching emptiness, just as the *Heart Sutra* does, many people misunderstood him, just as they also misunderstand the *Heart Sutra*. At one point, he was accused by the Buddhist scholars of being a nihilist. Most probably, some Buddhist teachers discouraged people from going to him, saying Milarepa was an emanation of Mara who would "corrupt your consciousness, take you on a wrong path, and doom you to a terrible place."

The funny thing is that the Buddhist tradition has the idea that someone may be an emanation of buddhas or bodhisattvas, or reincarnation of someone in the past. They are called *tulkus (sprul sku)*. And then there is also the idea of an emanation of Mara, which is the opposite of a tulku.

Negating Through Metaphors and Reasoning

Some people don't use this title for someone who is a thief or lowlife, but as a weapon for those who challenge their doctrine.

One time, Milarepa made a famous statement: "You'll know whether I'm a nihilist or not by looking at my actions." In other words, if he was a nihilist, he wouldn't believe in cause and effect, ethics, nonviolence, compassion, and so on. But Milarepa was harmless; he was like a saint and never harmed anyone once he entered the path. However, in the end, Milarepa was killed by a monk who sent poison to him.

Even though in the ultimate truth, Buddha himself challenged the doctrines, beliefs, and consensus reality of the world, he also said he would live in peace with the world, and go along with the consensus reality. Buddha said in a Mahayana sutra, "The world argues with me. I don't argue with the world. Whatever exists in the world, I also say that it exists."

Buddha is talking about the conventional, relative truth. He is not rejecting the relative truth. Let's say you and Buddha are driving together on the highway and there is a lot of traffic. Buddha wouldn't say there is no traffic, it's all illusion. He would go along with common reality and perhaps say, "Yes, there is a lot of traffic." If you say to Buddha, "We haven't eaten food for the last six hours. I'm hungry. Let's go to a restaurant," Buddha wouldn't say,

"There's no you, there's no me, there's no hunger." He would say, "Yes, let's go to a restaurant."

Emptiness in Relationship to Self and Other

We mentioned earlier that there are two kinds of emptiness, known as no-self of individual and no-self of phenomena. *No-self of individual* is emptiness in relationship to your own existence as an individual. It is negating the existence of an intrinsic self. *No-self of phenomena* is negating the intrinsic realness of everything that exists in this universe or in our mind's imagination, including nirvana.

In Tibetan, we call these *gang zak gi dag med*, (*gang zag gi bdag med*), no-self of individual, and *chö kyi dak med* (*chos kyi dag med*), no-self of phenomena.

They are the same emptiness, except no-self of phenomena includes emptiness of everything—emptiness of self, emptiness of buddhahood, emptiness of samsara, emptiness of nirvana, and so forth. In the realm of emptiness, even the realness of nirvana is transcended or negated.

By the way, you notice we are using many Tibetan words here and not Sanskrit. This is because many of the Mahayana Sanskrit scriptures have been lost. Today most of the Sanskrit scriptures exist either in Tibetan or Chinese. In many ways, the Tibetan translations were extremely faithful to the Sanskrit texts, so using Tibetan helps us trace back to the original meanings.

There are many reasonings to show or illuminate emptiness in relationship to self and to all things; that is, to negate the realness of self and everything that exists. Some of these reasonings are archaic, almost too philosophical. They may not make much sense to us anymore.

For example, if there is a thing that is real, then it has to be born. It has to be born from self or from other, or from both or from neither. So there are reasonings to prove that things cannot be born out of themselves, out of other, out of both, or out of neither. This logic gets so convoluted that you might like to work on it if you are having a hard time falling asleep. It is so unenticing that it really can work as a sleeping pill; you may save money on melatonin.

These two kinds of emptiness, the two kinds of no-self, are considered a fulcrum of the Mahayana tradition. But not all the Tibetan Buddhist traditions agree with each other on how to describe these two types of emptiness. Lama Mipham as well as Lama Tsongkhapa tend to say that no-self of person and no-self of phenomena are really not different in terms of their nature and what they negate, which is the intrinsic nature, or *svabhava*. However, for example, the Sakya school has a different way to describe the two types of no-self, drawing a hierarchy between them. We don't want to get into all the early philosophical differences, so for us, they are the same emptiness.

These two categories of no-self are very logical. They also have to do with the progress of awakening. For example, it may be difficult for individuals to suddenly wake up and realize that *everything* is empty of svabhava. That's harder to do. So maybe the first or most important stage that one comes across on the path to awakening is the realization of no-self of person. From that realization, one experiences freedom, non-attachment, letting go, and joy. Then one can stretch the scope of one's understanding and see that not only one's self but everything else is indeed empty of intrinsic nature, svabhava.

This is why it is important for the traditions to give a map of emptiness. Not because there are different kinds of emptiness, but so that we can wake up to the emptiness of everything. Otherwise we may let go of attachment to one thing but not to another.

We all have our own special illusion or dream that we are attached to, one we have a hard time letting go of, even when we can let go of many other things. That's why the traditional categories of emptiness can help us go through deep reflection. We have to inquire into everything, all that we can comprehend, and let go of grasping to all of them, seeing that they are lacking in *svabhava*, intrinsic nature. Things are not as real as they appear, so we gradually loosen our grasping, and our hope and fear in relation to them.

Negating Through Metaphors and Reasoning

Two Ways of Negating

Let's talk a bit more about negation. There are two ways of negating the apparent reality of everything. It seems that some of the early schools, such as the Nyingma tradition and many other Indian and Tibetan Buddhist schools of thought, tended to negate everything directly. Remember, they used a vase and pillar as the main objects of inquiry in the Madhyamaka texts. So there are some schools of thought that directly negate the vase. They say there is no vase.

Then there are other schools of thought, such as Lama Tsongkhapa's school, that say you cannot negate anything directly. You cannot say there is no vase. You must add this word *dön dam* (*don dam*), which means *in reality, in actuality*. So you have to say "there is no vase, in actuality." There is a vase, but there is no vase in actuality. They say if you don't add "in actuality" or the term *dön dam* in Tibetan, then your negation is not a meditation on emptiness; it is actually nihilism. You fall into nothingness.

There is a huge debate between the two schools of thought about this one topic. Of course, many other topics are debated, but this is one of the main ones.

Gendun Chöpel, who died in the 1950s, was one of the great Madhyamikas, perhaps the most famous Madhyamika in recent times. He said we should not add the concept "in actuality." He said we have to negate everything directly.

He thought if we add "in actuality," we will never challenge or shake our dualistic perceptions, because we have been believing everything to be real, to be the way we experience it, for so long. He said if we negate directly, it is so shocking and radical that it may loosen our attachment and grasping to the intrinsic realness of everything.

Gendun Chöpel's position is in alignment with many thinkers before him, such as Lama Mipham. Lama Mipham wrote a famous text when he was quite young, known as *Ngeshé Drönmé (nges shes sgron me)*, the *Lamp of Certainty*. In this text, he clarified the Nyingma philosophical position in relationship to Madhyamaka, and how it might be distinguished from other Tibetan Buddhist schools. In it, he also challenged many great thinkers and prominent scholars indirectly.

Lama Mipham presented a refutation in relation to the idea that when you talk about the emptiness of a vase, for example, you have to say the vase is "empty of svabhava of vase" or "empty of intrinsic nature of vase," not just "empty of vase." Lama Mipham felt that if you don't assert the emptiness of the vase, and just say it is empty of intrinsic nature, then you are never going to realize the emptiness of the vase, because you are not negating the notion of the vase directly. He felt that you must assert "vase is empty of vase."

Remember, in the end, there is no negation. Negation is also just another effort, a process to arrive at the *actual ultimate truth*—emptiness not as an absence of something but emptiness as nonduality. Yet for the yogi to arrive at the realization of a more nondual emptiness, she or he may have to go through the first process, emptiness based on negation. Eventually the yogi will outgrow negation-based emptiness. Then he or she is ready to realize the nondual emptiness, the actual ultimate truth.

Buddha himself spoke of both the negation-based emptiness and the nondual emptiness. In many ways, Buddha is a nondualist, even though we can't really put Buddha into any kind of category.

Empty of Intrinsic Nature

Let's go back to the last line we were working on: "In the same way, feeling, perception, formation, and consciousness are emptiness."

Basically, as a negation, *emptiness* means empty of intrinsic existence. There are many ways, using both analogies and reasoning, to realize emptiness, to realize that all things are empty of intrinsic existence. Hypothetically, if there is such a thing as intrinsic existence, intrinsic realness, then things can exist independently—a vase can exist as a vase, a pillar can exist as a pillar, there is good and bad intrinsically—without depending on or being contingent on what are called "words and concepts," *ming* (ming) and *tok pa* (rtog pa).

Ming literally means a name, but it really means to label, to name, to use words. And *tok pa* means concepts.

Let me share a quotation from a text known as the *Four Hundred Verses on Madhyamaka* by Aryadeva, a main student of Nagarjuna. In this verse, Aryadeva said,

> Whenever there are concepts, there is attachment.
> Without the concepts, there is no attachment.

Remember that attachment is considered a very powerful klesha, or mental affliction, which can be the force or fuel that perpetuates samsara.

This verse is often quoted by many Tibetan Madhyamikas to state that nothing really exists on its own as a thing until we label it through our concepts. In his commentary on this verse, Changkya Rölpé Dorjé explained that this verse refers to concepts that are repeatedly habituated in us without a beginning. Such concepts as "this is form, this is feeling" are habituated in us again and again and become in-born in our mental states.

There is an age-old analogy that Madhyamaka uses to show how we label things with our concepts and make something out of nothing. Imagine that you are walking in the darkness, where there is very dim light, and you come across a coiled object, which is actually a rope, but you mistake it for a snake. You get a pang of fear. The truth is that there wasn't a snake in the first place, but in your mind, it is a snake. The snake-ness is not to be found anywhere in that object, neither in the whole thing nor in its components, such as the shape of the rope, head, tail, middle. In the same way, as a human being, we construct the sense of "I" or self, based on our five skandhas. And yet when we inquire, there is no thing, "the self," anywhere in our five skandhas.

The traditional Madhyamaka inquiry invites us to look for the self in all the components of our body, such as the thirty-two teeth, twenty-one thousand hairs, twenty nails, three hundred and sixty different bones, blood, mucus, organs. We are supposed to come to the realization that neither one thing nor the whole thing is the self. If we have an idea somehow that the whole thing or one thing is the self, then Madhyamaka has a stockpile of logic that will tear apart our belief right there on the spot. You can learn the details of the refuting logic in the classical treatises, but we won't mention them here because it will take a long time.

Through our in-born habits, we label not just the self but everything. Let's look at this inquiry by applying it to something around here. We can choose any kind of object as a basis of our Madhyamaka inquiry. Earlier, we gave examples of inquiry with a vase and also with a table. Let's review it again.

What is a table? Is this thing a table? This is a table in some sense. But if we sit together and inquire into the nature of this table, we will not actually find this table.

There's no tableness. You will not find tableness in any of the parts of the table or even in the whole table. Any time you find tableness and use further inquiry, logic, and reasoning, you will not find any tableness. So this table, which we all agree is here and is real, only exists as a table because it is created or constructed by concepts and naming, or labeling.

So things are empty of intrinsic existence but do exist as "this and that." They exist as good and bad, perfect and imperfect, only because we label them as good and bad. They exist as "this and that" only because we perceive them as "this and that" through the deep-seated habitual tendency of *tok pa*, or concepts.

Nothing to Negate

Now you have a very good idea of what emptiness really means. Ultimately, emptiness is not about negating anything. It's just a way to loosen and let go of our grasping to everything as real. This is why Acharya Asanga said in his famous text, *Uttaratantra*,

> *In this, there is not a thing to be removed,*
> *nor the slightest thing to be added.*
> *It is looking perfectly into reality itself,*
> *and when reality is seen, complete liberation.*

Negating Through Metaphors and Reasoning

This is also the heart of Dzogchen. Lama Mipham, in his Dzogchen aspiration prayer, wrote:

*In this, you won't find anything to be removed,
nor conceive of what could be added or produced.
Dharmata is unstained by efforts to cut or cultivate:
May we arrive at the state that is spontaneously there!*

What we have just said can cause a little confusion in some people because we have been negating true existence as the principal way of understanding emptiness. The *Heart Sutra* itself is full of these negations, which are statements that negate true existence of all things. But now we are looking at emptiness from another point of view, which says there is nothing to be negated. This philosophical dilemma has, of course, occurred in the past and has been clarified very well by the masters of the past. If you read the works of Lama Mipham, he gave a very beautiful clarification as a way to solve this dilemma. In the realm of the ultimate truth or emptiness, there has never been intrinsic existence, and this why you can say there is nothing to negate in the context of the ultimate truth. What we are really negating is some kind of illusory or virtual reality that only exists as an hallucination of our innate ignorance, which serves as the root of samsara.

Hypothetically, imagine there has never been innate ignorance in our consciousness. Then the whole

Madhyamaka system would not exist in the world, since such an illusion would never have developed. So Madhyamaka is a contemplative system that just helps us undo the illusion that we somehow created.

Buddha himself, as well as the most authoritative masters, such as Saraha, Nagarjuna, and Atisha, always spoke of the nonconceptual meditative state, where we can be completely in touch with the ultimate truth, a state where there is nothing to negate and nothing to assert. Somehow, it seems some later Buddhist schools didn't get it. This kind of nondual, nonconceptual truth or even meditative state is well deciphered in the Nyingma tradition.

For example, the Nyingmapa masters, such as Longchenpa, tend to distinguish three different levels of meditative states, such as a child's approach, or beginner's meditation, *jipa nyer chökyi samten (byis pa nyir spyod kyi bsam gtan)*; the meditation of discernment of the truth, *dönrap jépé samten (don rab 'byed pa'i bsam gtan)*; and the meditation of the Tathagathas, *dé zhin shek gé samten (de bzhin gshegs dge'i bsam gtan)*. The last one is regarded as the nondual, nonconceptual meditation where one's consciousness is mingled or infused with the ultimate truth. When one dwells in such a meditative state, one's mind is not busy negating anything. One's mind in that moment is totally mingled with the ultimate truth, in which the illusions of true existence are completely absent.

12

Thus, Shariputra, all phenomena...

Thus, Shariputra, all phenomena are emptiness. They have no characteristics. There is no birth and no cessation. There is no impurity and no purity. There is no decrease and no increase.

Remember, Buddha is witnessing this profound dialogue; he is totally engaged with it as the witness. Avalokiteshvara is continuously expounding emptiness, not just emptiness of self but emptiness of everything. That's why in this paragraph, Avalokiteshvara said that all phenomena are empty of characteristics. *Characteristics* is similar in meaning to intrinsic nature. It refers to the idea that we think things have intrinsic characteristics, such as something is intrinsically red or intrinsically good or bad or intrinsically tall or short. Yet although we call something "red" or "car," it is not intrinsically "red" or a "car." Things only exist as separate unique individual entities because we label them, we name them, we conceptualize them as this and that.

This *Heart Sutra* verse is quite important. Many commentators of the past explained this paragraph as an illumination of the *Three Gates of Liberation*, or *namthar go sum (rnam thar sgo gsum)*. The three gates are emptiness, absence of characteristics, and absence of expectations.

This notion is common in many Buddhist traditions, yet each school has its own way of interpreting it. For example, in the lower Abhidharma, the three gates of liberation are somehow connected with the understanding of subtle aspects of the Four Noble Truths. In the Mahayana tradition, the three gates are just different ways of describing the three main qualities of the same great emptiness. The ultimate truth, which has these three qualities, is also taught in Vajrayana. For example, there's a symbol in Vajrayana called the *dharmakara*, which looks like a triangle. Its three edges symbolize the absolute, the truth that has these three gates of liberation.

The three gates of liberation are also used as a way of negating the true existence of all phenomena in any possible way. They negate the intrinsic nature of things in the present, right now, as well as their intrinsic cause from the past, and any intrinsic fruition of something they will become in the future.

Ground, Path, Fruition

In Mahayana, there seem to be various creative ways of interpreting the three gates of liberation. For example, these three gates can be used as a systematic way of negating the true existence of what are called the ground, path, and result. These three terms are the most important framework for any Buddhist philosophical system.

Ground usually refers to the overview of all reality. It can be the two truths (relative and ultimate truth), or tathagatagarba, or the five skandhas and twelve faculties, depending on the philosophical system that we refer to.

Path is the whole process of walking the spiritual journey, which involves spiritual practice. It can be, for example, the process of accumulating merit and purification of karma, or the two tantric stages of generation and completion, again depending on the context.

Result is the achievement one gains from walking the spiritual path. Depending on the school of thought, it can be the two *kayas*, or three kayas, five wisdoms, or *Vajradhara*-hood, or attainment of samyak-sambuddha, and so forth.

The first gate, emptiness, can be applied as a means to cut through the grasping toward the true existence of the ground. The second gate, no characteristics, can be applied as a means to transcend grasping at intrinsic characteristics of the path. And the last one, no expectations, can be applied as a means to transcend grasping to the aspiration, the fruition, or result.

Basically, these three gates are another expression of emptiness that leaves nothing to hold onto, nothing to grasp at. Once you transcend the intrinsic nature of the ground, path, and fruition, as well as grasping to them, then there's nothing to hold onto. This is very powerful because it does not just negate the intrinsic existence of phenomena but brings down the whole structure of reality that we think is real, in which we have placed so much hope and fear.

Commentators tend to align each line of this *Heart Sutra* paragraph with each of the three gates of liberation. For example, some commentators say the first line of this verse, "All phenomena are emptiness," refers to the first gate of liberation. The next lines, "They have no characteristics. There is no birth and no cessation. There is no impurity and no purity," refer to the second gate of liberation. "No decrease and no increase" refers to the last gate of liberation, absence of expectations.

Nothing to Hold Onto

Let's go into this *Heart Sutra* passage line by line. The first line, "All phenomena are emptiness," means that all phenomena are empty of true, intrinsic nature because nothing really exists the way our ordinary, unawakened mind perceives things, from the biggest phenomena such as nirvana, to the smallest, such as a table. These things only exist because we mentally designate them as nirvana or table; beyond that they do not intrinsically exist anywhere. That's why we say all things are emptiness.

"They have no characteristics" means that even though all things appear to be real, they have no realness on their own. In the context of other Buddhist doctrines, the word for characteristics in Tibetan, *tsen nyi (mtsan nyid)*, might refer to the idiosyncrasies of individual things. But in the Madhyamaka context, the word *characteristics* refers to "inherent characteristics"; that is, the intrinsic nature of something, or its realness. The characteristics of something are just projections of our own unawakened mind. The truth is that since all things are lacking in intrinsic nature, they are also lacking in intrinsic individual characteristics. The characteristics that we see are our mind's display. In the absolute, there are no characteristics.

When the verse says, "There is no birth and no cessation," we can also remember that Madhyamaka has all the logic to negate the notion that things are born in the first place. There are four possible ways of things being born: either they are born from themselves, born from other, born from neither, or born from both.

There are actually schools of thought in India, such as Samkhya, that taught that things are literally born from themselves. Many of the Buddhist realist schools perhaps taught that things are born from other. Then there are schools of thought that teach that things are born from both self and other. And there are schools of thought that teach that things are born from neither, such as the early nihilistic schools. Madhyamikas came up with reasoning to show contradictions in all the four possible births or manifestations.

On the one hand, things are obviously born, otherwise things would not exist, according to our usual perspective. On the other hand, if we really analyze how things are born, they are not born from the four possible causes. Rather, they arise from contingency on many causes and conditions. So if we analyze, we cannot find that things are born. And because they were never born, then there is no death. They will never come to an end because they were never born in the first place.

And if they were never born, there is also no increase and no decrease, and no stain and no stainlessness, no purity and no impurity. On the spiritual path, we are always trying to purify our kleshas, such as the three poisons. But these three poisons don't exist in themselves, in the way we perceive them. They only exist as a relative truth. We label them as inner obscurations, but in themselves, they don't have any intrinsic nature. They are all concepts in the ultimate sense. So the idea of enlightenment, being free from our inner obscurations, is just a mental construct, because when we inquire, we cannot find these obscurations, just as we cannot find the table. In the same way, the notion of decreasing and increasing our qualities is not true. The idea that we are decreasing our inner obscurations and increasing our love and compassion is only a concept and in the ultimate sense, lacking in intrinsic nature.

View and Conduct

It is very important to bear in our mind that this is not indicating there is no path. There are karmic obscurations that we obviously have to purify. There are also the stages of awakening. But the *Heart Sutra* is simply negating the intrinsic nature, not just of the path and awakening but of everything that exists. Of course, most people won't have a misunderstanding about this, but just in case, we want to make that clarification. It is possible some people can misunderstand emptiness and think that the *Heart Sutra* is rejecting everything literally.

There's a story about a man from Golok in the twentieth century who was supposed to be a meditator, and who killed a sheep for food, saying, "There is no 'you' to be killed and there is no 'me' to be the killer." This man definitely did not understand emptiness, or else he misused it. He used it to justify his action of killing the sheep so he didn't have to feel bad. This is a total misunderstanding of emptiness. There is a path, there is karma, and there is a process of awakening.

It is important not to mix up *view* and *conduct*. If you allow your conduct to follow your view, then you can fall into some kind of nihilistic path, denying reality, like this man did.

Guru Padmasambhava said, "Don't let your action follow your view." He also said, "Your view should be as vast as the sky, and your actions should be as fine as barley flour." What he meant is that our view of emptiness, or nonduality, transcends notions of right and wrong, good and bad, because that is the nature of reality. At the same time, while we can be free inside by holding such an outlook, there is still a relative truth, where there is right and wrong. This is why we should not misuse these transcendent views to justify our careless and unwholesome actions.

Many people throughout history must have had this idea in their mind: "Once you are awakened, once you realize absolute truth, such as emptiness, you can do whatever you want to do and you will never be bound. Nothing will bind you." This is illustrated, for example, in someone's question to Padampa, when Padampa (11th century) was visiting Tibet. Someone asked, "When you realize emptiness, can you be harmed by doing unwholesome deeds?" Padampa's reply was, "There will be no impulse or urge to do any unwholesome deed when you realize emptiness, because the realization of emptiness and compassion arise simultaneously."

Even though in the ultimate truth everything we believe is a concept, as human beings we must follow the guidelines of right and wrong. The standards of right and wrong can sometimes be established by consensus, which does not often come from wisdom intelligence. So the true way of establishing the guidelines or structure of right and wrong is to say that any action that arises from true compassion is right. When we act from a lack of compassion, then our actions may be derived from ill-will, hatred, selfishness, ulterior motives, and lack of sympathy. Perhaps this is what Padampa meant.

Radical Negation

The *Heart Sutra* is basically pointing out that almost everything we can think of or hold as sacred is proven to be empty of intrinsic nature, just as ordinary things are. This can be a very radical idea to many people because as spiritual or religious people, we are so steeped in ideas of progressing on the path, karmic purification, and attaining enlightenment. The sutra is pointing out that there is nothing that is too sacred to inquire into in order to discover it is empty of intrinsic nature. In English, the word *sacred* is often associated with God or the divine, at least in the Judeo-Christian world. In Tibetan, the word *dag pa (dag pa)* is the closest word to sacred. *Dag pa* means "flawless." Sacred means something is flawless; it doesn't have to be something associated with God or gods. In that sense, in the Mahayana tradition, when we practice reverence to the sacred, we don't have to think that there is some kind of intrinsic divinity that we are worshiping. We are revering the flawlessness and emptiness of everything.

Remember, this is not saying things don't exist. They do exist. They just don't exist with an intrinsic nature. If we think they don't exist, we can fall into some nightmare nihilistic world. Nagarjuna warned us that such nihilism is very dangerous. He said, "Eternalism leads you to joy, happiness; nihilism leads you to the lower realms." When he spoke of joy, he was only speaking of earthly happiness, not enlightenment. But he found that eternalism may have some merit, while nihilism has no merit. Nihilism is a complete rejection that may close the door to liberation.

13

Therefore, Shariputra, in emptiness...

> *Therefore, Shariputra, in emptiness, there is no form, no feeling, no perception, no formation, no consciousness; no eye, no ear, no nose, no tongue, no body, no mind; no appearance, no sound, no smell, no taste, no touch, no phenomena; no quality of sight and so on until no quality of thought and no quality of mind-consciousness...*

One of the most prominent Dzogchen masters in the twentieth century was Khenpo Ngakchung. When he was a young monk, before he became so renowned, he had the duty of serving tea to the monks in the monastery during a prayer gathering of continuous *Heart Sutra* recitations. While he was serving tea to an older monk, somehow he was a little clumsy, and the tea missed the cup and spilled on the old monk's lap. The monk got upset and said, "Don't you have eyes?" Young Khenpo was very witty and said, "Haven't we been chanting 'no eye' all day?"

Here in the *Heart Sutra*, we are continuously negating the intrinsic realness of all phenomena, such as the five aggregates, or *skandhas*; the twelve faculties; and the eighteen *dhatus* or eighteen elements or spheres. These are philosophical categories that encompass almost anything that exists.

Why does the *Heart Sutra* go to such an extent to negate all of them?

One reason is to indicate that everything is empty of true existence. Nothing is excluded. The whole world of phenomena—the big ones, the small ones, the gross ones, the subtle ones, everything—are equally empty of intrinsic nature. It is said that this is a process that not only negates the realness of everything that we experience through our deep-seated concepts but also negates the belief held by some schools in India that there is an intrinsic self residing in our body that can experience the whole world of phenomena—sight, sound, touch, taste—independently. So the twelve faculties and eighteen *dhatus* are negated in this verse. Avalokiteshvara is again illuminating the emptiness beyond emptiness of self, which is the emptiness of all phenomena.

Therefore, Shariputra, in emptiness...

This group of lines not only expresses mahashunyata, the great emptiness, but also describes the entire Buddhist philosophy on the relative truth, including the five skandhas, twelve faculties, and eighteen spheres. It would be worthwhile to go over these categories in more detail. They are explained in the Buddhist teachings such as Abhidharma. It is said that the reason Buddha explained all these categories of phenomena and our existence was to show that there is no self, no intrinsic self. Instead, everything comes into being through the interdependence of the five skandhas, twelve faculties (or *ayatanas*), and eighteen *dhatus* (or spheres or elements).

We have already learned the five skandhas or aggregates. The first part of this group of lines, "no form, no feeling, no perception, no formation, no consciousness," covers the five skandhas as well as the emptiness of them.

Twelve Faculties

Next we have the twelve faculties—faculty in Tibetan is *kyé ché* (*skye mched*) or in Sanskrit, *ayatana*. The twelve faculties are often divided into two groups: the six inner faculties and the six outer faculties. The six inner faculties are the eye, ear, nose, tongue, body, and the mind. These are more than just the physical senses that we typically call eye, ear, etc. Then the six outer faculties are form, sound, smell, taste, touch, and phenomena or mental objects.

It is more accurate to add the word "faculty" to the each of the twelve that we just listed: eye faculty, ear faculty and so on up to touch faculty, and mental object faculty. They are called twelve faculties because they are the doorway, the medium, through which the consciousnesses—eye consciousness, ear consciousness, nose consciousness, etc.,—arise and engage with their respective objects.

Eye faculty refers to a particular nervous system in the eye. Body faculty does not refer to the entire body but to the nervous system that goes through the body. Often it has the connotation of some kind of sensory faculty, but in modern language we can call it some kind of nervous system. Nose faculty is not just referring to the nose, but to a kind of nervous system that runs through our nose, which we can't discover with our ordinary eyes.

The early Buddhists understood faculties in a way that was similar to our understanding today of the nervous system, though not in as much detail. They came up with their own conceptual image of the nervous system since they had no MRI at that time to see inside. For example, they described the faculties like this:

- the visual or eye faculty is like an *umaka* (flax) flower
- the ear faculty is like a twisted roll of birch bark
- the nose faculty is like parallel copper needles
- the tongue faculty is compared to a crescent moon disc

- the tactile faculty is like the skin of the "smooth-to-the-touch" bird

These are the twelve faculties or *ayatanas*.

Eighteen Dhatus

Then we have the eighteen *dhatus*, which can be divided into three groups of six; the first two groups are the same as the *ayatanas*. There are six outer dhatus—form, sound, smell, taste, touch, and mental phenomena—and six inner dhatus—eye, ear, nose, tongue, body, and mind. The last six of the eighteen dhatus are the eye consciousness, ear consciousness, nose consciousness, tongue consciousness, body consciousness, and mind consciousness.

There is quite a lot of information to memorize. You don't have to know all of it as long as you get the general idea about the categories. When you read these paragraphs in the *Heart Sutra*, you can find all the philosophical categories, such as the twelve faculties and the eighteen dhatus.

14

No ignorance, no end of ignorance...

no ignorance, no end of ignorance up to no old age and death, no end of old age and death...

This passage and the next one complete the whole process of awakening to the great emptiness. Beyond this verse, Avalokiteshvara talks about the power and the blessings of awakening to the great emptiness. So we have quite a bit to discuss.

Interdependent Origination

These lines refer to the emptiness of the twelve links of interdependent origination, or *pratityasamutpada* in Sanskrit. It is known as interdependent origination, or interdependent arising, depending on how you translate it.

Interdependent origination, or *pratityasamutpada*, is taught in almost all the Buddhist schools of thought. It explains the creation and dissolution of the wheel of samsara; it describes how samsara successively comes into being as well as how we can be free.

The twelve interdependent originations are considered one of the universal foundations in the Buddhist teachings, transcending all the differences between Theravada, Mahayana, and Vajrayana. So it seems very important to go through the twelve interdependent originations in order to really understand the notion that this whole existence continues. Obviously we don't have to think that much about continuation. If we look around, we see there is continuation. There is not really a beginning of anything, and there is no end of anything, either. The beginning and end of something are just an illusion.

Whatever you like to call this entire continuing existence depends on your mood. Sometimes you feel this is samsara, other times you feel this is nirvana. It depends on your mood, doesn't it? Tantric Buddhism teaches that if you are awakened to the nondual great wisdom, then you can be in samsara but you feel you are in Akanishta, the highest paradise. But if you are not awakened to the great nondual wisdom, then you can be in some kind of Buddha paradise, but you feel that you are in samsara.

Either way—samsara, nirvana—this whole existence has no beginning. The beginning is actually an illusion according to Buddhist tradition. Existence has no beginning.

We believe there is birth and there is death, and we are afraid of death. We are constantly being attacked by anxiety, nervousness, day and night, by fearing the phenomenon called death. Milarepa said,

> *I went into the mountains out of fear of death.*
> *I meditated and meditated on the unpredictability of death.*
> *Then the fear of death was lost.*
> *Now I have arrived at the primordial citadel*
> *of deathlessness.*

Birth and death only exist in the realm of the small self. The one who is born is actually the illusory self. The one who is going to die is actually the illusory self. In oneness, in the inseparability between you and everything, no one has been born and no one is going to die. It's like saying there is birth of eternity and death of eternity. Can that be possible? It's like saying there is birth and death of the universe. The universe and eternity have no birth, no death, no beginning and no end either.

But there is a continuation. We can call it continuation of the cosmos, or transmigration. How does it continue? This continuation of samsara has no beginning and yet its development has been described by the twelve interdependent originations.

Even though the twelve interdependent originations have an order, starting with ignorance, this does not mean that there was a time when there was no samsara and then everything happened after that. Often our rational mind wants to find the beginning of everything, such as finding the time when the universe was created by finding the big bang. Even if we don't know the beginning of something, we think we will discover it someday if we analyze it.

For example, in Christianity, original sin began when Eve ate the apple after listening to the serpent. This is a beginning, and there is a belief that it happened at a specific time. But did it? St. Augustine comments that when someone once asked another theologian, "What was God doing before he created this world?" the theologian facetiously answered, "He was busy creating hell for people who ask this question." But St. Augustine added that he himself would not say that, since it is all a mystery. So although we say samsara begins with *avidya*, really samsara has no beginning.

There are twelve stages of samsaric development, beginning with avidya, or in Tibetan, *ma rigpa*, ignorance or lack of understanding.

The twelve links of interdependent origination, *ten drel chu nyi (rten 'brel bcu gnyis)*, go like this:

1. Ignorance – *ma rigpa* (ma rigpa, Skt. *avidya*)
2. Mental formation – *du jé* ('du byed, Skt. *samskara*)

3. Consciousness – *nam shé* (*rnam shes*, Skt. *vijnana*)
4. Name and form – *ming dang zuk* (*ming dang gzugs*, Skt. *nama-rupa*)
5. Six sense faculties – *kyé ché druk* (*skye mched drug*, Skt. *sadayatana*)
6. Touch or contact – *rek pa* (*reg pa*, Skt. *sparsha*)
7. Feeling or sensation *tsor wa* (*tshor ba*, Skt. *vedana*)
8. Craving – *sé pa* (*sred pa*, Skt. *trshna*)
9. Grasping or attachment – *len pa* (*len pa*, Skt. *upadana*)
10. Existence or becoming – *si pa* (*srid pa*, Skt. *bhava*)
11. Birth – *kyé wa* (*skyed ba*, Skt. *jati*)
12. Old age and death – *ga shi* (*rga shi*, Skt. *jara-marana*)

As we said, the twelve interdependent originations, or twelve *nidanas*, can be found in both Theravada Buddhism and Vajrayana, including Dzogchen, so it is a very important category. In general, all the Buddhist lineages teach pratityasamutpada, or the twelve links, as a continuation of existence, so their ideas are similar to each other. Yet they all have their unique way of interpreting it. For example, Vajrayana describes the successive development of samsara through the language of the *nadis*, *prana*, and *bindu*; they incorporate those three elements into the twelve interdependent originations.

Pratityasamutpada is a complete theoretical framework, or construct, or map that explains how things come into being and how things continue to exist; it includes our own transmigration, the whole world, and suffering. Pratityasamutpada also gives us an idea of how suffering can be reversed in order to alleviate it.

Some aphorisms in the Buddhist teachings explain pratityasamutpada as "Because this exists, that exists. Because this doesn't exist, that doesn't exist." So pratityasamutpada is also a teaching or an understanding of the law of cause and effect. The law of cause and effect can be very positive, dealing with happiness, freedom, awakening, and sometimes less positive, dealing with suffering, ignorance, etc.

A Meditation

The twelve interdependent originations are also a meditation in the Buddhist tradition. We say there are two ways of meditating on interdependent origination. Those on the path of seeking liberation for themselves meditate on pratityasamutpada by becoming aware of how their own existence continues, how suffering comes into being, and also how it can be transcended. So they begin to see their own liberation through this meditation.

The Mahayana Buddhists meditate not only on their own samsara but on the samsara, the twelve interdependent originations, of all living beings. Through such contemplation, one can be so moved that one gains a very strong determination, an aspiration, to bring about the liberation of all living beings. These two ways of meditating on interdependent origination are taught particularly in the Mahayana texts.

There are also two methods used in the meditation on interdependent origination. The first is the successive order in which one realizes that all the links follow one after another in order. For example, from ignorance, formations come, then consciousness arises, etc. Another method is the reversal, in which the meditator seeks to see how samsara comes into being. He or she asks, "Where does old and age death come from? They come from birth. Where does that come from?" and so on, tracing all the way back to ignorance.

Either way, the contemplation on interdependent origination is considered so vital that the Tibetans often not only meditate on the whole system of interdependent origination but they also recite this Sanskrit incantation almost all the time:

Om ye dharma hetu prabhava hetun,
tesham tathagato hyavadat,
tesham ca yo nirodha, evam vadi maha shramana. Svaha

The translation says,

Of all things that arise from a cause
The Tathagata has said, "This is their cause,

And this is their cessation."
Thus the Great Shramana teaches.

This mantra is known as the essence of pratityasamutpada and is used to bless the beginning of the day, any endeavor, weddings, laying foundations for construction, and so forth. Tibetans recite it all the time in the Tantric sadhanas, as well. This mantra describes the Four Noble Truths because interdependent origination explains the cause of suffering as coming from ignorance, from karma and kleshas.

Tibetan temples also have the image of the Wheel of Existence, which visually describes the twelve interdependent originations.

The Endless Chain

Let's go through the twelve links one by one.

The first is *avidya*. What is avidya? In general, avidya means not knowing. In Sanskrit, *a* is a negative particle and *vidya* means knowledge. Here we can understand avidya as a delusion that arises from not knowing the true nature of reality, a delusion in which we believe in the true existence of self. We grasp at the illusion of self as real. We believe in the true, intrinsic existence of everything else as well. Grasping at self and the true existence of everything is avidya.

Yet avidya is a very vast topic and there are different interpretations of it. Vajrayana and Dzogchen further extend the understanding of avidya. Tibetan Buddhism is a synthesis of all the Buddhist teachings, so we have access to different teachings on the same topic from schools of thought that no longer exist in India. Some Tibetan scholars point out the differences between the definitions of avidya in all the different schools of thought.

However, regardless of the different definitions, the first of the interdependent originations is avidya. If we interpret interdependent origination as the successive way that samsara comes into being, then out of that ignorance, samsara continues to develop.

What happens next? Then there are *mental formations*, or *samskara* in Sanskrit, *du jé* (*'du byed*) in Tibetan. *Du jé* here means mental formations but is also similar to karma. There are three kinds of karma, or *du jé*: advantageous karma, disadvantageous karma, and unmovable karma. Unmovable karma is karma that cannot be easily erased, such as the positive impact of meditation.

Then, as we continue this development, *consciousness* arises. We need consciousness to carry everything. Consciousness is the force that carries our karma, our habits, memory, all our mental accumulations. It refers to a particular state of consciousness that carries and ripens the seeds of samsara.

Next are *name* and *form*. Form is the first skandha, *rupa skandha*, and name refers to the other four skandhas.

The *six sense faculties* refer to the faculties for our six senses, like eye sense, nose sense, ear sense. We went through these earlier.

Touch or *contact*, *sparsha* in Sanskrit, is what happens when, for example, you touch an object. *Sparsha* means that consciousness, your faculty, and the object come together. When they meet, there is sparsha.

Feeling or *sensation* is very easy to understand. It arises from touch. Remember, there are three kinds of feelings: pleasant, unpleasant, and neutral.

When there is feeling and sensation, then there is *craving*. There is craving for pleasure and craving to be free from the unpleasant. There are also three categories of craving in association with the three realms of existence: the cravings in the realm of desire, the cravings in the realm of form, and the cravings in the realm of formlessness.

There are also other categories of three cravings such as craving for pleasure, craving for nonexistence, and craving for existence. The first one is our desire to experience what is pleasant, such as joy, happiness, sensual pleasure. The second one is craving to be free from the unpleasant. The third one is the craving for this samsara to continue through our ego-identification. Craving for existence is more than just instinctual desire. Your desire to exist is natural, it is uncontrived. Craving is more like a neurotic level of desire, almost a neurotic obsession. That craving usually is accompanied by a lot of fear and insecurity, including fear of death.

Then *grasping* and *attachment* arise. The difference between craving and grasping is that you can simply have a craving without acting on it, but with grasping, you indulge in the craving. You start really engaging with your craving, seeking to totally identify with the object that you are craving.

Existence, or *becoming* means that all your engagement becomes very potent, very powerful, and results in a force that can now continue the cycle of existence. In Sanskrit, this is called *bhava*.

Birth, the eleventh link, is very easy to understand. And the twelfth link is *old age and death*.

The twelve interdependent or dependent originations, or the twelve *nidanas*, are a description of all the karmic, physical, and mental forces that continue this transmigration.

Here I'm using the word *transmigration*. We can use another word, but transmigration means that whatever we regard as ourselves—this being-ness, this existence—is a traveller, a cosmic traveller that transmigrates, that continues to flow, that goes from here to there.

The twelve interdependent links can be broken into three categories. Some of the links belong to the forces that brought you into this current manifestation. Some of them describe your current state of your being. Other links describe conditions that lead you into the future, or future existence. So the twelve links describe everything—the past, present, and future—about this whole existence, which connects with transmigration. This is one way of understanding the twelve links.

Interdependence and Ego Identity

Other teachers, such as Buddhadasa, explain interdependence differently. Perhaps many modern people in the Western world respond well to Buddhadhasa's interpretation. He was a Theravadin monk from Thailand who passed away in the 1990s and today is revered as a great teacher and thinker. But he was more than a great teacher and great thinker. He was what we might call a pioneer, a founder of a whole new paradigm. He distanced himself somewhat from the Thai Buddhist establishment, went on his own, and studied the sutras thoroughly for a long time. He became well-versed in all the Buddhist teachings beyond Theravada. Some people think he is a wonderful link between Theravada and Mahayana Buddhism because he brought many of the Mahayana Buddhist concepts into his writings.

Buddhadasa introduced the twelve interdependent links in relationship to self-concept. He said the twelve interdependent links are continuously happening every day. This is a totally different interpretation, isn't it? He said the twelve interdependent links are a way of understanding how the self-concept comes into being. Self-concept refers to the notion of a personal self. So he interpreted interdependent origination as the karmic links that describe the process of how this egoic identity comes into being. In that sense, he said, the twelve links of interdependent origination are happening all the time.

Buddhism also uses the theory of interdependent origination not only to explain how things come into being but also to negate the notion of a Creator. Because things are happening from causes and conditions, there is not one single Creator doing it all.

The good news about these teachings is that there is not one way to interpret them. There is not just one way as the "only way." This is the beauty of many of the Buddhist teachings.

In this verse of the *Heart Sutra*, Avalokiteshvara is saying there are not even the twelve links of interdependent origination. So here you can see Avalokiteshvara is expounding emptiness on many levels, all the way to the level of nonduality. This turns out to be a very radical teaching. Let's go further.

15

No suffering, no cause of suffering…

no suffering, no cause of suffering, no cessation of suffering, and no path; no wisdom, no attainment, and no non-attainment.

These lines are negating the Four Noble Truths. It turns out to be very radical to declare that there are no Four Noble Truths. The Four Noble Truths are considered the underlying foundation of all the Buddhist teachings. Yet in the *Prajnaparamita Sutras*, Buddha is declaring that just as there are no "twelve interdependent arisings," there are also no Four Noble Truths, and so forth.

This is why the Mahayana sutras, especially the *Prajnaparamita Sutras*, had a difficult time being accepted when they first emerged in India. Most Buddhists did not accept them as authentic scriptures; perhaps many of them thought that Nagarjuna and his followers just made the whole thing up. Many Buddhists were challenged by statements such as the emptiness of the Four Noble Truths. They may have felt like a wealthy person who just found out that the government devalued the currency and everything he counted on was worthless, gone.

When you have a chance, you might like to read the debate that went back and forth between orthodox Buddhists and Mahayana Buddhists on the subject of emptiness. Orthodox Buddhists basically said the whole set of Mahayana teachings, especially the Prajnaparamita teachings, were completely baseless and did not capture Buddha's wisdom. The orthodox Buddhists could not accept mahashunyata, the great emptiness, the teaching that everything, including the Four Noble Truths, is empty of true existence. This is why there is a recurring theme in many Mahayana Buddhist writings that asserts itself as the authentic teaching of the Buddha.

One time, even the great masters Acharya Asanga and his brother Vasubandhu had a big conflict. At first, Vasubandhu was a follower of Vaibhashika, one of the two early Buddhist schools of thought. In the beginning, he was an opponent of Mahayana, and even criticized his brother's alignment with Mahayana. This illustrates that there was a great deal of division in Buddhism in India, along with rejection of the Mahayana doctrine, mostly its doctrine of the great emptiness. Later, however, Vasubandhu himself became a strong follower of Mahayana.

In this verse, the *Heart Sutra* is teaching that there is not one single thing that is not empty of its true existence, including the twelve interdependent arisings, and even the Four Noble Truths. As we said earlier, in the Mahayana tradition, you are invited to question and inquire into the true nature of everything. There is not even one single thing that you should not inquire into, even the true nature of the most sacred, such as buddha nature, *tathagatagarbha*, and *dharmakaya*. It means that everything that you can comprehend in your mind is illusion, is empty of true existence.

No Attainment

In this verse, "attainment" refers to buddhahood, or the idea that one has been wandering in samsara and finally attained the perfect buddhahood. In the Mahayana, it would mean attaining the *four kayas*. In Theravada it would mean attaining *arhatship*. Attainment is what all the Buddhists are looking for. To attain *samyak-sambuddha* is more or less the goal of the entire spiritual path.

There are also *siddhis* as attainment. The Tantric tradition talks about the supreme siddhi and ordinary siddhis. It has the famous eight ordinary siddhis, including the ability to perform miracles. The supreme siddhi is the true authentic spiritual awakening.

So the entire Buddhist tradition is filled with the idea that there is something to be attained. It is true that there is something to be attained; there is enlightenment, there are siddhis. Yet here the *Heart Sutra* is transcending all of these along with everything else. When we inquire into their nature, we cannot find anything to hold onto. They are empty of true intrinsic nature, just like everything else.

The *Heart Sutra* is saying these attainments are a kind of mental construct that we created. This is important because the whole point of the *Heart Sutra* is to make sure that we don't get attached to notions such as enlightenment or attainment. For example, on the bodhisattva's path, one of the things that one has to purify or abandon is attachment to the buddhas and buddhahood. We can get attached to the buddhas and buddhahood when we reify them.

In the famous Mahayana text *Abhisamayalankara,* the *Ornament of Realization,* revealed by Acharya Asanga, he lays out the list of inner obscurations a bodhisattva must overcome. One line says, "The subtle attachment to the buddhas." This kind of attachment to the buddhas is considered a subtle form of dualism that a bodhisattva must overcome. The *Abhisamayalankara* also gives ways to overcome it, such as meditation on emptiness.

In our ordinary, conventional context, we also have a sense of attainment, such as success, education, achievement. If people go to one of the Ivy League schools, they may feel they have a great attainment. But we can see that people suffer a lot when they have attachment to attainment. They can develop pride and identify with their attainment. It becomes a hindrance for their inner spiritual development.

In the Chöd tradition, there are four Maras or inner demons who bind us. They are known as the Mara of the tangible, the Mara of the intangible, the Mara of elation, and the Mara of self-conceit. We can see that some of these Maras can control us when we completely buy into attainment. For example, we could easily fall prey to the Mara of elation. We feel happy and elated because we think we have achieved something. It is okay to be elated, but if you think that it is really real—you and your achievement are real—then you are deceived. That experience of elation is not stable, and then when you lose it or you lose your status, you suffer.

This is not to say there is no attainment. There is attainment in the spiritual world as well as in the ordinary world too. But the *Heart Sutra* is saying that if you look deeply into all these attainments, in the end, they are just a mental construct. If there were no mind in the first place, there would be no attainment. Our mind has to create this notion of attainment. This simple logic reveals that attainment is as empty of intrinsic nature as anything else. Some may be shocked by this declaration. But don't worry, this is not an outright rejection of attainment. It is just saying that attainment is not as real as it appears when we deeply inquire into its foundation or nature.

No Non-Attainment

The verse says there is "no attainment and no non-attainment." Non-attainment is the idea in Buddhism that there are sentient beings wandering in samsara who haven't attained enlightenment. This is the state of samsara—not attaining buddhahood. Yet from the point of view of Prajnaparamita, this is just a concept, too. There is no non-attainment. This is kind of radical because some Buddhists are attached to the idea that there is samsara, there are deluded sentient beings aspiring to be enlightened some day, and there are the stages of enlightenment, or bhumis. So here the *Heart Sutra* is saying non-attainment is also just a concept if you inquire deeply into it.

Emptiness of non-attainment is important because in our ordinary world, people believe there is non-attainment, and that without an attainment, they are a failure, they are losers. This idea causes a great deal of internal agony, self-doubt, or self-hatred. In our human world, we are always competing and comparing ourselves with each other. When we are told we haven't "made it," we feel we are inadequate, incompetent. We construct a poor image of ourselves and are harsh on ourselves, thinking, for example,

"All my siblings achieved something; my younger brother got married, my younger sister won some kind of award. I haven't attained anything." This comes from believing in the intrinsic reality of non-attainment. However, we can transcend all of this.

All the evaluation of ourselves through the idea of attainment and non-attainment of enlightenment causes so much mental conflict, but it is all based on an existential delusion about who we are. Buddha said that almost everything that we think about ourselves is completely erroneous. He said, "Those who hold views ... such as 'I am better than others,' 'I am equal to others,' or 'I am worse than others' are those who do not see things as they really are."

A Glimpse of Emptiness

I feel this whole idea of emptiness is not just a philosophical concept. Again, it is just a way of letting go, loosening our grasping to the realness of everything.

Maybe you have already had a glimpse or taste of emptiness in your life without even connecting it with Madhyamaka or the *Prajnaparamita Sutras*. We sometimes can see that intrinsic realness is an illusion because we constantly go through a lot of changes in our own consciousness. We think of something as good right now, but later we may change our mind. We may think of something as bad and then may end up seeing it as very good in the future. Good and bad are not intrinsically solid.

In the same way, you may have the experience of relating to somebody who you think is repulsive or not a good person, and then someday you realize that person is actually wonderful; you may end up liking that person. Have you ever had this kind of experience in which your perception has changed fundamentally in the course of your life? So even our moral ideas are always changing. Our idea of what is real is not permanent; it is always changing. So you see, realness is an illusion. *Svabhava* is constantly discrediting itself in our everyday life; even if we are not meditators, if we just pay enough attention, we will see the illusion.

What is perfect? What is imperfect? What is good? What is bad? What is valuable? What is not valuable? What is sacred and what is not actually sacred?

We all think that this Tara statue next to me is sacred. At least many of us think that this Tara statue is sacred. For many people, this statue would not be sacred, it wouldn't even be Tara. Many people have no idea who Tara is. This is one of many examples where we can see that everything is empty, none of our ideas are absolute and unchanging.

Once upon a time, a famous Gelugpa geshé and his friends decided to debate with Gendun Chöpel when they heard he had returned from India. The geshé wanted to revenge his defeat by Gendun Chöpel in the early years. So they went to see Gendun Chöpel. The moment Gendun Chöpel saw them coming, he picked up his beloved statue of Buddha. He was smoking a cigarette and started dropping ashes on the statue. This completely freaked them out; this was like blasphemy for them. They then started debating this topic, arguing that what he did was very bad. Gendun Chöpel quoted a line from *Abhisamayalamkara* that describes the enlightened attributes of a Buddha: "They taste the unpleasant flavors as delicious." Somehow he defeated all of them in the debate. Gendun Chöpel was not being disrespectful; obviously he had great reverence for the statue. But he was pointing out the emptiness of everything in order to shock everyone's mind.

In the end, when we turn our attention inward and start questioning our perceptions again and again, we realize all our perceptions are temporary, conditional, and often given by society, given by the outside world.

Loosening Attachment

When we think things are intrinsically real, we develop grasping and attachment. There are two kinds of attachment. You can call them negative attachment and positive attachment. "Positive" here does not mean good. Positive attachment is when you want to possess, own, or hold onto something. Another kind of attachment is negative attachment, when you want to get rid of or reject something. Negative attachment is what we usually call aversion, but it is attachment because we are attached to our own idea of something as being repulsive or negative.

Someone told me that there are sanghas who chant the *Heart Sutra* all the time as the main liturgy. They use a method from time to time where they add a phrase in the *Heart Sutra* during the negation. Let's say you are attached to or really obsessed with something, such as a nice car or good job. Then you can add that object as one of the negations that say "no this" and "no that." This can be a wonderful practice. We might like to think of something we are really attached to and put it in the *Heart Sutra*. We don't have to say it out loud in front of everybody. We can say it in silence.

We can say "no this" and "no that" because whatever we are attached to does not have any kind of intrinsic reality. The very object we are attached to is just another phenomenon. But our dualistic mind makes it more real, more concrete, than it is. Our mind tends to concretize whatever we are attached to, either as extremely enticing or extremely repulsive. As we just said, attachment can take two forms—one wants to hold on and another wants to reject and destroy.

So it would be helpful if you added one or two phrases whenever you chant the *Heart Sutra*, a phrase that works with your own attachment, whatever that might be—an object of attachment that is somehow holding you back from evolving, making your consciousness smaller, or making you suffer. It can be some kind of object or material acquisition that you are really attached to. You may not have it yet or you may already have it.

It doesn't even have to be a material or tangible thing. Maybe it can be hatred, if you hate somebody. Or you can put in something abstract, something non-material, such as nirvana. If you are attached to nirvana, you can use nirvana, which is actually already in this verse: "No wisdom, no attainment."

Even if these teachings on emptiness, especially Madhyamaka and all the reasonings, don't make sense at first, they will help us to loosen and let go of our attachment to everything. At some point, after you have been practicing the reflections on the great emptiness, you are going to experience that you are able to let go of—if not completely, then at least soften and loosen—your obsession and grasping to all the things you are attached to.

That's why these teachings say everything is illusion. Everything that we love or hate is all illusion. Things do exist to a certain extent, even though they may not exist the way we perceive or experience them. Indeed, sometimes the definition of relative truth is explained in Tibetan as *né nang mi tün pa (gnas snang mi mthun pa)*, that which has dissonance between the way it appears and the way it is. And the definition of ultimate truth is *né nang tün pa (gnas nyang mthun pa)*, that which has harmony or resonance between the way it appears and the way it is in reality.

When we start inquiring into everything, maybe things don't go away. It's not as if everything suddenly becomes unreal. But things become less real than the way we have been holding onto them. So the idea that everything is illusion—using the teachings and the practices to negate the existence of everything—is not pointing out that everything is totally nonexistent, like some kind of nothingness. In some sense, everything is real. This is why we are here. We can smell, we can taste, we can touch, we can experience. There is me, there is you, there is a whole world. So everything is actually real in some sense.

Ultimately, Madhyamaka or Prajnaparamita teachings—whatever we like to call them—are not really trying to teach us to think that everything is nonexistent, everything is illusion, everything is completely empty. These are all just methods to simply cut through our grasping to the way we experience everything.

Usually we don't inquire unless we are part of the yogi's world. We don't inquire into the true nature of anything. This is why we are attached to everything as real. Once we start inquiring into the true nature of everything, then we become part of the yogi's world, as Shantideva said. Then we begin to see the falsehood of our own perceptions, our own beliefs, our own attachment, and then maybe we lose our attachment to a lot of things. But it does not mean we are going to wake up and see everything as empty or nonexistent. I think this is a very important point to make.

A Lifelong Practice

The Prajnaparamita teaching is not some kind of knowledge we can study for a while and gain mastery over. It is a lifelong practice we should engage with. It is said that it is almost impossible, or very difficult, to arrive at the complete awakening to nonduality unless you go through the process of negation. We might like to wonder whether or not the negation-based practice is in our own spiritual path.

If we don't have this kind of negation, divine negation—we should add the word *divine*—then even if we are on the spiritual path, we may have what they call merit, *punya*, but we may never wake up. Not only that, we may be developing a lot of attachment, a kind of beautiful attachment. In other words, our spiritual path may be just another beautiful samsara. But it is still samsara. There are many things we can get attached to, even on the spiritual path.

Let's say you are really attached to nirvana. Maybe not too many people are attached to nirvana these days, so this may be a poor example. But let's say you are really attached to nirvana and now you are doing the Prajnaparamita practice; you are meditating and negating the realness of nirvana. Even though there is nirvana, you may be able to let go of your attachment to nirvana. In the beginning, we may need to be attached to nirvana in order to be inspired. But in the end, we may need to drop that attachment as well. Maybe we can be attached to nirvana as we long as we don't fall into the delusion that it has some kind of intrinsic reality.

Sometimes when people are attached to nirvana, they are not really attached to nirvana but to their preconceived notions of nirvana. People then miss the point and fall into the duality of sacred and secular, true and untrue, and can get quite deluded. They also forget to practice love and compassion toward the human condition that is right in front of them. Their attention is lost in their lofty ideas. So, attachment to nirvana can be tricky if people are attached only to their own ideas of nirvana.

I'm not saying that attachment is always negative, but if we are not mindful, it can be very messy or tricky. In general, attachment may be part of being human. But there are moments when attachment can become unhealthy if we are not mindful, not inquisitive enough. When we inquire, we know which attachments are healthy and which are unhealthy, which ones bind us and which ones are benevolent.

In the end, this whole practice—the meditation on emptiness—is to cut through our dualistic perceptions. In the realm of emptiness, everything is the same in its essence. There is no good, no bad, no ordinary, no holy. This practice is immensely profound, but sometimes you feel that anything you say about it becomes limiting and conceptual.

16

Therefore, Shariputra, since the bodhisattvas...

Therefore, Shariputra, since the bodhisattvas have no attainment, they abide by means of transcendent wisdom. Since there is no obscuration of mind, there is no fear. They transcend falsity and attain complete nirvana, passing beyond the bounds of sorrow.

All the Buddhas of the three times, by means of transcendent wisdom, fully and clearly awaken to unsurpassable, true, complete enlightenment.

These verses praise Prajnaparamita, or the truth of the great emptiness, as the path that all the bodhisattvas undertook. The verse says that all the buddhas of the past, present, and future were bodhisattvas at one time. As bodhisattvas, they practiced the Prajnaparamita path and awakened to the great emptiness. Through this realization, they became *samyak-sambuddhas*, completely, perfectly awakened ones. They conquered their own fear and purified their consciousness of inner obscurations. As we said earlier, Prajnaparamita is praised as the "Mother of all the Buddhas" because all the buddhas are born from this realization. Now Avalokiteshvara is encouraging everyone to practice the Prajnaparamita.

The first paragraph of this verse is connected to what we just discussed about transcending the whole idea of attainment. Now Avalokiteshvara describes a kind of bodhisattva's meditation where bodhisattvas abide in the nondual awareness, nondual wisdom that is free from all the *trö pa (spros pa)*, all the mental proliferations.

These lines are also saying that the bodhisattvas have purified their consciousness of all forms of inner obscuration holding them back from embracing the authentic full awakening. *Obscuration* can be defined in many ways. For example, when somebody goes through the different grounds of awakening, there are obscurations that he or she has to purify one by one at each stage. Obscurations can refer to them.

Obscuration can also refer to the two obscurations known as the obscuration of internal afflictions and the obscuration of knowledge. The first obscuration refers to the internal afflictions or emotional obscurations that hinder one from attaining liberation. The second obscuration hinders one from attaining *samsaksambuddhahood*.

In the *Uttaratantra*, there is a verse that defines these two obscurations:

*Thoughts such as stinginess and so on,
these are the emotional obscurations.
Thoughts that involve the three-fold subject, object, and action,
these are the cognitive obscurations.*

In short, anything that prevents us from awakening can be regarded as an obscuration. In some sense, everything we do on the path can be regarded as a means of purification. This is why all the spiritual practices in the Buddhist tradition can be synthesized into two points: cultivating wholesome accumulations and purifying obscurations. You could say all the spiritual practices fall into these categories, no matter how profound or how insignificant they might be.

Yet it is true that some practices are more powerful techniques for purifying obscurations than others. For example, meditation on emptiness is a more powerful method for purifying obscurations compared to reciting sutras for days without any understanding, even though that recitation has its own merit. In Tibet, people turn prayer wheels as a way of accumulating wholesome virtues and purifying inner obscurations. Of course, this practice has merit as long as the intention is correct. There is blessing in it. Yet there is no doubt that meditating on emptiness is a more powerful means than someone turning a prayer wheel without deep insight.

Once somebody asked a famous scholar from Amdo, Arik Geshe Chenmo, "How does it work that turning the prayer wheel can cause buddhahood?" He said, "The truth is that the prayer wheel is just a sacred scripture in a yak skin. What we really need is an understanding of what those texts say. If someone doesn't understand them, then at least they can study, contemplate, and meditate on the teachings expressed in the texts. Those who can't do that can just recite those scriptures. If someone can't do that, then at least they can turn the prayer wheels." His humorous anecdote explains there is some hierarchy in the purifying power of spiritual practices that we do; they may not all be the same.

Going back to the verse, "no fear" means that the bodhisattvas have conquered their fear of embracing emptiness. Remember, emptiness is supposedly the most frightening thing to many people since it shatters all their illusions. By making friends with and meditating on emptiness, one can awaken and let go of fear. Fear is almost like the hallmark of existence.

"Falsity" in this verse can be regarded as our mistaken perceptions, our delusions, in relation to the true nature of reality. The Mahayana tradition talks about four kinds of mistaken perceptions: seeing the impure as pure, seeing suffering as happiness, seeing the transient as permanent, and seeing no-self as self.

These categories of mistaken perceptions may be different in Vajrayana, which is all about celebrating the whole phenomenal world, the entire manifestation, life itself. In Vajrayana, we might say the mistake is not seeing everything as sacred. We can say that to see everything as sacred is the true perception.

In any case, falsity means we see wrongly through our own deluded mind; we don't see things as they are. This verse states that bodhisattvas go beyond the host of all delusions. Eventually bodhisattvas achieve the perfect enlightenment, *samyak-sambuddha*.

17

Therefore, the great mantra...

Therefore, the great mantra of transcendent wisdom, the mantra of great insight, the unsurpassed mantra, the mantra that equals the unequaled, the mantra that calms all suffering, should be known as truth, since there is no deception.

The mantra of transcendent wisdom is said in this way:

Tadyatha Gaté Gaté Paragaté Parasamgaté Bodhi Svaha

Thus, Shariputra, the Bodhisattva Mahasattvas should train in the profound transcendent wisdom.

The first paragraph in this verse is quite easy; it is praising the power of the Prajnaparamita mantra. But we must realize that this mantra is not some kind of holy incantation that we can recite to exorcise the army of Mara, all the negativities. Here, the entire mantra is a practice of Prajnaparamita. A mantra is a kind of axiom that captures volumes of teachings, and the Prajnaparamita mantra encapsulates the hundreds of volumes of *Prajnaparamita Sutras* and teachings. The mantra is an aphorism synthesizing all the Prajnaparamita teachings.

As we said earlier, you can even shorten the mantra so that it is eventually only one syllable, *Ah*. We can use *Ah* as the shortest mantra of the Prajnaparamita teachings, symbolizing the unborn, deathlessness, the great emptiness. So this verse is not just praising the one mantra, *Gaté Gaté Paragaté...*, it is praising all the wisdom and profundity expressed in the *Prajnaparamita Sutras*.

The verse says, "This mantra is the mantra of transcendent wisdom." *Transcendent wisdom* means the highest wisdom, beyond the worldly wisdom. It is the awakened mind, emptiness. This mantra is inviting us to meditate and to realize the great emptiness.

"The mantra of great insight" refers to the mantra of wisdom that can transcend and purify our primordial ignorance as well as all the habitual tendencies, which are the very root of samsara.

"The unsurpassed mantra" is saying that the wisdom of Prajnaparamita is the ultimate medicine to cure our illness, the suffering of samsara. They say there is no method or wisdom higher than this. It is like the queen of all the wisdoms.

"The mantra that equals the unequaled" means enlightenment is ultimate freedom, which is unequaled. Nothing can compare to it. This mantra allows us to realize it, to actualize the great awakening that is unsurpassed. Nothing can be equaled to it, so it says "equals the unequaled."

"The mantra that calms all suffering." This line is quite important. There is a tradition called *zhi jé* (*zhi byed*) brought to Tibet by Padampa Sangye, who was Machig Labdron's guru. They say even the name for the *zhi jé* lineage comes from this one line, "The mantra that calms all suffering." *Zhi jé* in Tibetan means that which calms or pacifies.

This line is quite easy. It means that the transcendent wisdom has the power to pacify our suffering, its causes, and its habitual continuation, and to lead us to inner liberation.

"Should be known as truth, since there is no deception" means this mantra is the expression of the ultimate truth. This wisdom is the ultimate truth that we can completely trust and take refuge in as the sole source of inner liberation. The verse is encouraging us to have trust. With our trust, all the qualities of the Prajnaparamita teachings just described have the power to awaken us, liberate us from our suffering, and lead us to ultimate freedom.

Om Gaté Gaté

Om has many meanings. Om means blessing, grace, auspiciousness, divine. Tantric Buddhism adds the syllable Om at the beginning of all the mantras. It is said that once you add Om, it blesses the whole incantation as a mantra. Then they often add *svaha* as another sacred word that makes the entire phrase a mantra. That's why in our chant, we add Om at the beginning and *svaha* at the end.

Tadyatha means thus. When we recite the mantra by itself, we usually recite it just as Om Gaté Gaté Paragaté Parasamgaté Bodhi Svaha. But some Tibetan commentaries say that you have to recite both *Tadyatha* and *Om: Tadyatha Om Gaté Gaté Paragaté Parasamgaté Bodhi Svaha*. Some commentaries say these are all fabrications and you don't have to add those extra syllables. In the *Heart Sutra* sadhana composed by Nagarjuna, he says you should add Om.

Some commentaries associate this mantra with the five paths. The five paths are like a Buddhist map showing the gradual stages of awakening:

1. The path of accumulation (Skt. *sambharamarga*)
2. The path of engagement (Skt. *prayogamarga*)
3. The path of seeing (or insight) (Skt. *darshanamarga*)
4. The path of meditation (Skt. *bhavanamarga*)
5. The path of no-more-learning (Skt. *ashaikshamarga*)

Therefore, the Great Mantra...

Although the five paths have to do with the process of inner awakening, awakening happens on the third path, when you experientially see the truth of emptiness. The first path, the path of accumulation, is where you exert the noble effort that accumulates the cause for such awakening, for seeing the truth. The second path is the path of engagement. Here, even though you don't see the truth directly, you are very close to it. You are really ready to go there. The third path, the path of seeing, is where you see the truth. The fourth path is meditation, where you habituate yourself with what you've seen. When you have finished, and there is nothing more to be trained, there is nothing more to learn, you have reached the last path.

You can interpret the first *Gaté* as going to the path of accumulation, the first path. The second *Gaté* means going to the path of engagement. Then the third word, *paragaté*, means going to the path of seeing. *Parasamgaté* means going to the path of meditation. *Bodhi* means the last path, the path of non-learning. There's nothing to learn; you've become enlightened. The last path, *bodhi*, is the great awakening.

Svaha here means "May it become so" or "May I attain awakening."

This is the end of Avalokiteshvara's teaching. Now, in the Tibetan version of the *Heart Sutra*, there is an ending passage.

18

Then the Blessed One arose...

Then the Blessed One arose from that samadhi and praised noble Avalokiteshvara, the Bodhisattva Mahasattva, saying, "Good, good. Thus it is, O son of noble family, thus it is. One should practice the profound transcendent wisdom just as you have taught, and all the Tathagatas will rejoice."

When the Blessed One had said this, venerable Shariputra and noble Avalokiteshvara, the Bodhisattva Mahasattva, that whole assembly, and the world with its gods, humans, asuras, and gandharvas rejoiced and praised the words of the Blessed One.

This is a typical way of ending all the Mahayana Buddhist sutras, not just the *Heart Sutra*. Almost all the sutras have a similar beginning and ending, although the locations are different, and sometimes the students and individuals who initiate the dialogue are also different. But the structure is similar.

Here Buddha praises Avalokiteshvara and says, "The way you taught is correct." In that sense, they say even though the *Heart Sutra* was not spoken by Buddha, it can be regarded as a sutra. It can be attributed to the Buddha and his teachings because Buddha blessed the whole dialogue.

So this is what we call "the grand finale." Everyone is happy. This is the end of the *Heart Sutra* as well as the end of all the *Prajnaparamita Sutras*. This grand finale offers a beautiful and benevolent image as we imagine that all the beings—the humans, the gods, the gandharvas, the spirits, the extraterrestrial folks—have understood emptiness and were liberated. This is such a nice image to invite into our own consciousness. It's a very hopeful image where there is no suffering, no infighting, no confusion. Everyone, all these beings from different realms, are happy and awakened.

It would be nice if the whole human world could reach this kind of harmony, awakening, and peace among each other. Even though maybe people think this ending is just a drama, it is a profound message to all of us when we dive deeply into it. This tells us that we can all come together, regardless of who we are, regardless of our race, social class, background. We have so much potential together to take care of the weak, to protect the environment, and to make sure we take care of Mother Nature for our future generations. We can stop fighting, war, and sectarianism. We can accomplish so many good things if we put our differences and fighting aside. We see that many of our problems come from divisions with each other, which often have to do with our attachment to our ideologies. We think our ideas are right and everybody else is wrong. We have zero tolerance when somebody criticizes our ideology. This is how sectarianism and many wars come into being.

The *Heart Sutra* is encouraging us to let go of our ideas, to go into the heart, and to see the big picture. As John Lennon said, "Some say that I'm a dreamer, but I'm not the only one..." There are a lot of bodhisattvas out there who feel the same.

The Experience of Emptiness

Recently, someone posed the question to me: "What is emptiness?" What happened was very interesting. In that moment, I didn't have any answer. Then I realized, I'm writing a book on emptiness, so I'd better have an answer! The answer that arose in me was rather unpredicted. It wasn't very logical. I said that you can feel the great emptiness if you can drop all your thoughts for a while, which means dropping all your perceptions: the good ones as well as the bad ones. Just drop all of them.

If you have a moment in which you literally drop all your perceptions— perception of good, perception of not good, perception of right and wrong—if you drop all of them in a single moment along with all your thoughts, then there is a wide open awareness in which you can hear, think, touch, taste.

There is still a world out there. It is not as though everything dissolves. The world is manifesting with wonder, magic, and amazing vibrancy. It feels as if everything is so alive. But you can't say, "Oh, this is good. This is beautiful. This is ugly." You don't have the words to describe any kinds of limitations or characteristics. You feel this aliveness, this amazing vibrancy, the wonder of existence, and the wonder of being alive. That's what emptiness is.

It is the experience of yourself, your world, your surroundings, of people, of everything, the totality, without any limited perception. That's really what emptiness is.

Once you are able to experience emptiness—to feel your life, to feel the magic, the pulse, this wonder of life and everything, without any limited perception—you can practice what they called in Tantric Buddhism *dak nang (dag snang)*, pure perception. *Dak* means pure, sacred. And *nang*, in this case, means perception, by which you begin to see that there is sacredness in everything.

Then the Blessed One arose...

All-Pervasive Sacredness

It is said that once you're awakened to mahashunyata, the great emptiness, you can finally experience true all-pervasive sacredness. Until then, you can never really experience all-pervasive sacredness because you'll somehow be holding onto the realness of everything, which is your own mental obscuration or mental fabrication. All-pervasive sacredness is emptiness. It is empty of all limitations; it is empty of duality, empty of flaws. If you think that sacredness is different from emptiness, that is a form of duality. Emptiness is not a nihilistic nothingness. Emptiness is actually rich and full. It is the depth, the wonder, the mystery, the inexpressible aspect of everything, of reality.

When you realize the great emptiness, you will lose attachment, you will lose fear. Then you can open your consciousness and experience the all-pervasive sacredness, which is the idea that form, sound, and your internal experiences are all equally sacred. You experience the world as a mandala, all sounds as mantra, and all your thoughts as a play of the awakened mind, the buddha mind.

It is said that no teaching in Buddhism, especially in Mahayana and Vajrayana, should stray from the realization of emptiness. Therefore, the wisdom of Vajrayana is just another expression of the great emptiness. This is why all the mandalas and deities are considered different expressions of emptiness. In Vajrayana, we use the images as skillful means in order to experience love and devotion to emptiness. Avalokiteshvara is an expression of emptiness who is kind, loving, and who gazes upon all living beings with a compassionate eye. Vajrayogini is an important expression of emptiness who is described as very alive and dynamic. The female deities in Tantric Buddhism especially symbolize the great emptiness because they give birth to awakening. They symbolize wisdom, the wisdom of the great emptiness.

In the end, this whole teaching is really a way to lose our attachments to our own ideas and concepts about anything that we can comprehend.

19

Emptiness with Compassion-Essence

Nagarjuna is considered both a Mahasiddha and a pandita, but he's also a mystic. When I say mystic, I mean somebody who is not attached to any concepts. He influenced many traditions—Buddhism as well as Hinduism. He said something extremely profound that synthesized the heart of all the wisdom traditions. He said there are three very important principles for anybody who wishes to actualize enlightenment or awakening.

In one of his verses, he wrote,

If you and the world wish to attain
unsurpassable enlightenment,
its roots are bodhichitta,
unshakeable like Meru, the queen of mountains;

compassion that reaches everywhere;
and wisdom not relying on duality.

In the Mahayana teachings, both the wisdom of emptiness (*prajna*) and compassion (*karuna*) are very important. They are like the two wings of the bird. Mahayana teaches that their integration is indispensable for the inner awakening, for those who are ready to realize the highest truth.

As we conclude the *Heart Sutra* and its teachings on emptiness, I cannot imagine a better time than now to talk about the other wing of the bird, compassion, the awakening of the heart. I like the expression "awakening of the mind and heart." We also need to open our heart. From that point of view, enlightenment is not just that we wake up inside and feel our consciousness is illuminated or that we figured out something profound. It is more about opening our heart through love and compassion. Guru Padmasambhava said, "The root of your spirituality is rotten without compassion." This is a very powerful statement. The root of your spirituality is rotten without compassion.

Compassion is more than a nice concept, more than some kind of good moral concept. It is almost as though we need it in order to continue our path. We need compassion for our own sanity, for our own happiness, and for the happiness of the whole world and humankind. Without compassion, we may feel that this world is cold and unfriendly. We may feel that our whole being, our consciousness, is contracted and frozen. Compassion has the power to melt all the "inner frozen" and bring about a sense of connection with humanity.

Our Innate Impulse

Compassion is, of course, intrinsic to each of us, an innate impulse. Compassion is not something we have to learn how to feel. We already have this impulse as our innate gift. Compassion is our basic impulse.

If someone, perhaps a teacher, says, "There is a Buddha inside you" or "The Divine is inside you," what do you usually find when you turn your attention inward? Do you find something extraordinary and sublime inside yourself? If we understand what this teacher is pointing out, we would feel in touch with our innate love and compassion. Maybe we can say this is buddha nature, this is our inherent goodness.

There is inherent goodness, but what is that? If you don't know how to point it out, it can be one of those very nice, uplifting phrases that makes us happy. I call this a kind of spiritual placebo. Words have the power to affect our psyche whether they are valid or not. Thinking there is inherent goodness can make us feel really good, but that is not the point. I think we have to find out exactly what our inherent goodness is. The idea is very abstract if we don't say, "This innate compassion, this innate love or kindness or innate courage is the divine within me. This is the innate goodness I possess as my inborn gift."

We naturally feel this innate compassion. We always say, "I hope all of humanity is going to be okay. I hope all the deer in the forest are going to be okay. I hope the fish in the ocean are going to be okay. I hope the polar bears in the North Pole are going to be okay." This is really how we feel many times in our ordinary life, even though we may not be meditating or doing anything that is a spiritual observance.

Four Immeasurables

I like the expression that Einstein used, "widening the circle of compassion." We already have compassion as our own buddha nature. Our practice, our assignment, is to learn how to widen and expand the circle of compassion. This is where some of the traditional practices can be extremely useful, such as the Four Immeasurables. The Four Immeasurables are immeasurable love, immeasurable compassion, immeasurable sympathetic joy, and immeasurable equanimity.

The practice of meditating on the Four Immeasurables is a method to keep widening our love and our compassion. Immeasurable here means that you are expanding the circle of love and compassion from just a single individual or a few people to an immeasurable number of living beings.

Emptiness with Compassion-Essence

Sometimes they hold this notion in Mahayana Buddhism: "Wherever there is sky, there are sentient beings. Wherever there are sentient beings, there is sorrow." You imagine that the sky or space is limitless and is pervaded by an immeasurable number of living beings. You imagine in your mind that there is sorrow wherever there are sentient beings, and you learn to include all the immeasurable number of sentient beings in your heart, in your love, in your compassion.

There was a great Kadampa lama named Khampa Lungpa, who went into the mountains and cried all day. When people asked him, "Why are you crying all the time?" he said, "Because I am aware of the all-pervasive suffering of humanity and this world."

Later someone visited Khampa Lungpa's master, Dron Tönpa. Dron Tönpa asked the visitor, "What is my student so-and-so doing?" The visitor said, "He is busy teaching the Dharma to hundreds of people."

The master said, "Wonderful. And what is my other student doing?" The visitor said, "He's doing very well. He is building a lot of stupas and statues."

Again the master said, "Wonderful. And what is my third student doing?"

"He does nothing but meditate."

"Wonderful," the master repeated. Finally Dron Tönpa said, "Tell me what Khampa Lungpa doing?"

The visitor said, "He doesn't do anything. He just goes into the mountains and cries all day."

At that moment, Dron Tönpa joined his hands by his heart. He was moved to tears and said, "Ah. That's extraordinary. That is the true practice of Dharma."

Expanding the Circle

Even though we do have a lot of challenges in modern times from inside as well as outside, scientists are finding that overall, humanity is evolving, we are becoming more and more compassionate. In other words, the circle of our compassion is expanding as part of our evolution. This is very good news.

In the old days, most people didn't think much about other people beyond their family members or their tribe. But now we actually think about a lot of people, even people on the other side of the globe. We are sometimes quite sincere and passionate about the well-being of people whom we have never met, whom we have no cultural, political, or religious affiliation with. We don't just ignore their suffering, their struggles. We feel their suffering in our heart, in our veins.

During a meditation retreat that I led in Korea a few years ago, one woman said, "I'm feeling so much sadness about what is going on in Syria." To me, that was the best sharing report. I felt that she was having an authentic awakening, true bodhichitta, even though she presented it in such ordinary language. It was so moving to see that somebody in South Korea was deeply concerned with the well-being of people in Syria, which is very disconnected culturally from Korea.

The meditation retreat in Korea was held at a monastery located in the outskirts of the modern city of Seoul. While I was walking around in the corridor of the temple, I saw some magazines and flyers in the Korean language. One flyer caught my attention. Some Buddhist organizations were coming together and going to other parts of the world, such as Africa, to help people. I saw a picture of Korean monks and nuns in their gray robes helping people somewhere in a small village in a third-world country. Seeing this demonstration of pure love and boundless compassion made me optimistic about humanity and our future.

It doesn't really matter whether you go somewhere to help people or not. The point is not to stay contracted inside, not to stay finite, but to keep evolving into the infinite. Many mystics say that in the end, the spiritual path is a journey from the finite into the infinite, or from the conditioned to the unconditioned. To me, infinite means the infinite in ourselves, the infinite compassion, the infinite love. It is moving away from being very narrow into being expansive, from being frozen into melting.

Yet we may never arrive at the moment when we can say, "Now I reached the infinite." We can never say, "Now my heart is fully opened; I cannot open it any more." There won't be a moment when you can say, "Now I feel my consciousness is so expanded, there's no more place to expand any more." This moment will never happen. They say the universe is constantly expanding. So our heart can continuously expand.

True Transcendence

Some say the whole religious or spiritual impulse that we have is our longing for transcendence. Here, true transcendence is not so much about just transcending the self; it is not so much about waking up and thinking there is no more self. Maybe that can happen, but good luck with that! It would be nice if we woke up and said, "I see myself as an illusion, I don't exist any more. So it doesn't matter what happens to me. I'm happy because there's no me." That sounds very tempting, but I am starting to question that version of transcendence.

To me, the true transcendence is not so much about transcending yourself or the duality between yourself and others. It is true that the duality between oneself and others is ultimately an illusion. But it is always going to be there. As long as we live in this form, in this incarnation, there is some kind of duality that we can't pretend does not exist.

Emptiness with Compassion-Essence

True transcendence is not that we wake up and see that duality is an illusion or just see "self" as illusion and completely transcend it. It is about expanding our heart, widening the circle of love and compassion, and connecting more and more with humanity, connecting with all living beings, with all the creatures that exist. Feeling connected with all the beings that we can see and that we cannot see, including insects, fish in the water, lobsters, crocodiles—you can name them. And not just feeling connected but that you are connecting with a tender heart. You actually begin to experience their suffering. This is true transcendence.

Whenever we feel our heart is open, connecting with something bigger than ourselves, with other people or humanity, with all living beings, we feel truly free inside. We feel happier than ever.

Moving to the Infinite

Let's learn to expand the circle of love and compassion. This morning you can hold one person in your heart. But this afternoon maybe you can hold many people. Tomorrow maybe you can hold a thousand people in the circle of your love. It is possible that the day after tomorrow you can hold many, many people in the circle of your love and compassion. This amazing shift can happen within a short period of time. Within just one meditation session you can go having from a closed heart, being self-absorbed, into an amazing bodhisattva who is holding and embracing all living beings in one circle of love and compassion. That kind of powerful shift can sometimes happen at any moment.

As we continue expanding the circle of love and compassion, we feel we are becoming more and more infinite. Can you feel it? You are becoming more infinite. You feel you are going away from the finite, step by step, and moving toward the infinite, step by step. You feel you are moving away from the conditioned toward the unconditioned, step by step. You feel that the circle of your happiness, your joy, your bliss, is also expanding, too. You feel that you are becoming greater inside.

20

A Daily Practice

The Prajnaparamita path is a practice; it is not just a theory. The question is, how do we practice this?

Let's talk about the role of the *Heart Sutra* and *Prajnaparamita Sutras* in our daily practice. There are many longer *Prajnaparamita Sutras* that could be used for daily practice. But if we don't use those, at least we can chant the *Heart Sutra* as a way to practice the Prajnaparamita in everyday life.

Having a philosophical understanding of emptiness can be extremely beneficial. At the same time, that is not enough unless we have some kind of practice as a means of letting go of our attachment to everything, to all of our concepts. Whether you have a very rich knowledge of the *Heart Sutra* or not, you can still practice chanting the *Heart*

Sutra to experience the whole process of dropping all your illusions, dropping your concepts.

The truth is that there is no such thing as a rich knowledge of the sutra. You can spend the rest of your life perfecting your conceptual knowledge of the *Prajnaparamita Sutras*. So whatever knowledge you have is perfect in itself, because you can never say, "Now I have complete conceptual knowledge of Madhyamaka or the *Prajnaparamita Sutras*." You can keep reading all the texts and books, and thinking and contemplating, and gathering more information and more logic. It's an unending process. So please don't worry about whether or not you have some perfect conceptual understanding of the *Prajnaparamita Sutras* or the *Heart Sutra*. Whatever understanding you have is perfect in itself.

We might like to recite the *Heart Sutra* more as a prayer, a sacred liturgy, to experience letting go—letting go of our attachment, letting go of things that are binding us. It doesn't matter whether we are thinking about what emptiness means or not. Sometimes we don't think or contemplate when we recite the *Heart Sutra*.

A while ago, somebody gave me a book called *Street Zen*, about the life of a Western Zen Buddhist teacher who died from HIV. This Zen teacher kept reciting the *Heart Sutra* after he was diagnosed with HIV. In his biography, he said that the only thing that kept him going, that kept him strong, and that helped him to keep his spirit up, was this simple chanting of the *Heart Sutra*. This is an inspiring story for the lovers of this sutra like myself. Perhaps if we can remember to recite this sutra in times of difficulty, we might be able to let go of hope, let go of resistance, and experience pure surrender. Maybe we will be able to see life as just an amazing play of emptiness.

There is a sense that when we are deeply immersed in the wisdom of emptiness, then nothing can really throw us off balance. This is because we see everything—whatever exists in our life—as a play of emptiness, and don't take things too personally or too concretely. This kind of inner freedom is described in various Mahayana teachings as well as in the *Prajnaparamita Sutras*, where it says:

Emptiness cannot find any way to harm emptiness.
No characteristics cannot find any way to harm no characteristics.
No expectations cannot find any way to harm no expectations.

This kind of inner freedom is not some kind of brilliant philosophical proposal. There are many people in the past who experienced this kind of extraordinary inner freedom, not just in some fuzzy spiritual state but in the face of life's challenges. While there are different ways people find joy and equilibrium when they go through a crisis, awakening to emptiness is one of the best remedies because it teaches us not to reify situations, not to make them more solid than they are.

Many people who are not part of the yogi's world may experience emptiness naturally when they go through a big loss. At least then they have the opportunity to taste what emptiness is like, especially if they lose something they are really attached to. It forces them to surrender to what is and drop their concepts, ideas, preferences, and their usual paradigm of reality. When they finally give up their hope and resistance, then they experience emptiness a little bit, just a sample—an emptiness sample.

When you drive through Napa Valley in California, there are a lot of places where you can stop and taste a little sample of wine. When you go to grocery stores, there are sometimes a lot of cheese samples. So there is an emptiness sample, too, when you lose something in your life. When you want to get something and find you can't get it and you have to let go of it, that's an emptiness sample, a shunyata sample. But it is only a taste.

Other than that, unless they are on the path of inquiry, most people don't have the chance to experience emptiness. So emptiness may seem to be very grand, very abstract, but it is a liberating wisdom we can all access if we have the courage. On the path of awakening to the great emptiness, we intentionally hold courage and devotion, and basically let go of our attachment to our concepts and our ideas.

A Daily Practice

True Spiritual Practice

In the realm of emptiness, there are no more limitations. In the end, it is not about negating anything. In the phase of negating, we negate duality, and we negate the existence of self. It's true that many practitioners go through this phase of negating, or trying to transcend something... transcend the self, or negate the existence of self. Then we can become very attached to the idea of no-self.

Ultimately in the experience of emptiness, nothing is being negated, not even the self. We are freed completely from any kind of conceptual ideas. Self is not negated. Duality is not negated. In the realm of emptiness, there is self, there is me, there is you. There is everything—there is life, there is joy, there is sadness—everything.

Yet there is also a deep knowingness inside you that you are no longer any of these: you are no longer your history, you are no longer your personal image, you are no longer your gender, you are no longer your illusion of self. You are no longer all these egoic identities, even though they are there.

You are no longer this ego. You are this inexpressible emptiness that has no limitations and is indescribable. You can't describe the emptiness of yourself. It has no shape, it has no color, it has no size. It is completely ungraspable, beyond words and measurement. When you have a moment to see that clearly, then you can say that you saw your original face, the Buddha within you. Finally you know who you are. That is the highest form of self-knowledge. There are many levels of self-knowledge, but to truly realize the emptiness of your own self is the true self-knowledge.

The highest form of spiritual practice is to abide in that again and again. Abide in that emptiness within you again and again. That is awareness. That is true awareness practice, to practice abiding in that realm within you, the emptiness within you.

A Final Reminder

Thank you everybody. This seems to be a perfect time to end. We have been listening to the dialogue between Shariputra and Avalokiteshvara. Now the teachings on the great emptiness are complete.

A final reminder: all this negation of everything—the five skandhas, the karmic law of cause and effect, all the way to wisdom and nirvana—is not to be understood as outright rejection and denial of their existence. That would be nihilism. Emptiness is not nothingness. In the relative truth, there is everything: five skandhas, cause and effect, wisdom, nirvana. Yet from the point of view of Prajnaparamita, ultimate truth, there is nothing we can hold onto. This is what true emptiness is—nothing to hold onto.

A Daily Practice

Now we can say,

The sun is rising from the shoulder of the Eastern Mountain.
A few clouds are moving with such grace.
Birds, animals, people, are ready to start their day.
How unbearably beautiful this life is.

About the Author

Anam Thubten grew up in Tibet and at an early age began to practice in the Nyingma tradition of Tibetan Buddhism. He is the founder and spiritual advisor of Dharmata Foundation, and he teaches widely in the United States and abroad.

Anam Thubten's published books in English include *No Self, No Problem*, *The Magic of Awareness*, and *Embracing Each Moment: A Guide to the Awakened Life*.

More information about Anam Thubten, including his teaching calendar, can be found online at <u>dharmata.org</u>.

www.ingramcontent.com/pod-product-compliance
Lightning Source LLC
Chambersburg PA
CBHW071155070526
44584CB00019B/2798